AF540519

ACADEMIC AUDIT

By the Same Author

— Governance and Management of Technical Institutions
— Management of Competency Based Learning
— Competency Framework for Human Resources Management
— सीखने की विधियाँ (Learning Methods)

ABOUT THE AUTHOR

Dr. B. L. Gupta is Professor in Management at National Institute of Technical Teachers' Training and Research, Bhopal. He completed B.E. in Civil Engineering in the year 1982 from SGSITS, Indore. He completed LL.B. from The College of Law and Legal Aid Shahdol in the year 1988. Then he completed Master of Technical Education in the year 1992 and Ph.D. in 2002 from Technical Teachers' Training Institute, Bhopal. Professor Gupta has 27 years of experience in the field of teaching, training and consultancy. He is trained in Great Britain. He has received training from well-known personalities of the country. He has conducted more than 460 management development programmes for various clients such as teachers of technical institutions, trainers and managers of industries. He has guided more than 15 theses in the field of technical education and management of industries. He has published more than 50 papers in national and international journals. He has developed variety of print and non-print instructional material for teachers, managers, officers and employees of various organisations. He is a visiting faculty for a number of training institutions of repute. He has worked on various World Bank Assisted Projects. Earlier to this book he has written seventeen books.

ACADEMIC AUDIT

B.L. Gupta

Professor, Department of Management
National Institute of Technical Teachers' Training and Research, Shamla Hills, Bhopal-462002
badrilalgupta72@gmail.com

CONCEPT PUBLISHING COMPANY PVT. LTD.
NEW DELHI-110059

ISBN: 978-81-8069-737-1 (HB)

First Published 2011

Published and Printed by

Concept Publishing Company Pvt. Ltd.
Regd. Office:
A/15-16, Commercial Block, Mohan Garden
New Delhi-110059 (India)
Phones : 25351460, 25351794, *Fax* : 091-11-25357109
Email : publishing@conceptpub.com
Website: www.conceptpub.com

Editorial Office:
H-13, Bali Nagar, New Delhi-110 015, India.

Cataloging in Publication Data--*Courtesy:* D.K. Agencies (P) Ltd. <docinfo@dkagencies.com>

Gupta, B. L. (Badrilal), 1960-
Academic audit / B.L. Gupta.
p. cm.
Includes bibliographical references (p.) and index.
ISBN 9788180697371

1. Universities and colleges--Auditing. I. Title.

DDC 378.11 22

Preface

For long the higher and technical education institutions have been searching for sound base for assuring, sustaining and improving the quality of graduates and other products and services but have been working on traditional systems. In the past decade some significant work on academic audit has been done in selected institutions. However, requisite literature was not available in the area of academic audit. To fulfil this need of the higher and technical institutions seemed to be the need of the time. Hence, the author considered it necessary to pen such a book.

This book particularly addresses the long felt needs of quality assurance, system design, academic audit and quality improvement at system and processes level in educational institutions. It also addresses the quality assurance needs of the governors, directors, head of departments, teachers, curriculum development cells, learning resources development cells, training and placement officers, statutory body, accreditation agency, and policy makers. It will enable the education managers to plan, design, implement and evaluate the educational systems at institutional level.

The author has used the relevant information from various disciplines, without defining and describing the concepts and principles. The readers are suggested to refer the relevant literature if they have further interest in related disciplines of quality assurance. Based on the long experience of the author in the field of technical education, many concepts, principles, models, procedures, tools, techniques and strategies necessary for assuring, sustaining, improving and innovating quality of education have been suggested in this book. It is for the readers to exploit the full potential of this book. The approach here is not to rename the traditional academic audit as academic audit but it is completely new, different and unique.

The book is not intended to point out the strengths and weaknesses of current quality systems in educational institutions. However, along with the useful inputs, enough guidelines to develop and implement each concept and ample activities with references to academic audit are provided in this book. It is left to the readers to use the formats and diagnose the strengths and weaknesses of the educational programmes.

Since the author has a long experience of designing, implementing and evaluating quality processes for technical education systems, government departments and corporate sector, the book reflects the views expressed in various training programmes and other fora. The author records acknowledgement to discussions and ideas of Prof. S.R. Ganorkar on academic audit. The long discussions with Prof. Ganorkar resulted in refinement of ideas and models on academic audit. In this context, the author records acknowledgement to the participants of various training programmes and industry personnel whose opinions, suggestions and ideas helped the author to conceptualize various models and strategies to publish this much needed book.

The author sincerely records acknowledgement to the Chairman and members of Board of Governors, Director and the faculty members of National Institute of Technical Teachers' Training and Research, Bhopal for their cooperation.

B.L. Gupta

Acknowledgements

This book on 'Academic Audit' is the outcome of many precedent training experiences and research studies conducted in past. I wish to record my sincere thanks to following persons :

Ex Principals and Directors of National Institute of Technical Teachers' Training and Research, Bhopal for providing opportunities to get international exposure.

Director, National Institute of Technical Teachers' Training and Research, Bhopal.

Prof. S. R. Ganorkar for free and open discussion on academic audit during implementation of training programmes.

The research scholars and their guides for conducting the research studies on topics related to their interest.

My colleagues at National Institute of Technical Teachers' Training and Research, Bhopal for openly sharing the experiences.

Library staff of National Institute of Technical Teachers' Training and Research, Bhopal.

My father Shri Shriniwas Gupta and mother Mrs. Sushila Gupta for sharing everything. My wife Mrs. Suman Gupta, sons Kumar Gandharva, Kumar Gaurava, and my niece Swati Suneria and Meera Farkya for supporting me during writing work.

Shri Ashok Kumar Mittal, Concept Publishing Company Pvt. Ltd., New Delhi for publishing this book.

Contents

List of Figures, Exhibits and Formats

List of Figures

List of Exhibits

List of Formats

List of Abbreviations

AA – Academic Audit
AS – Academic System
AAS – Academic Audit System
NBA – National Board of Accreditation
NAAC – National Assessment and Accreditation Council
AAM – Academic Audit Manual
ISO – International Organization for Standardization
SWOT – Strengths, Weaknesses, Opportunities and Threats
LRs – Learning Resources
LRDC – Learning Resources Development Centre
CDC – Curriculum Development Centre
BOT – Build, Operate and Transfer
LRUC – Learning Resources Utilization Centre
UGC – University Grants Commission

How to Read This Book

This book on *Academic Audit* is written which can be read in anyway the reader wants, depending on his/her interest. The book is equally useful for the new as well as experienced professionals. In totality, it deals with quality assurance, sustenance, improvement and innovation through academic audit. The whole book is divided in to nine chapters.

Chapter 1 describes overview of academic audit. Chapter 2 describes the process of audit—the vision. Chapter 3 describes process of audit—the organisational structure. Chapter 4 describes the process of audit—the plans. Chapter 5 describes process of audit—the curriculum. Chapter 6 describes process of audit—the case method. Chapter 7 describes the process of audit—the industrial training. Chapter 8 describes the process of audit—the learning resources and Chapter 9 describes the process of audit—the performance appraisal system.

The beginning of each chapter informs the readers about the abstract of the chapter. If the learning needs of the readers match with the abstract they must sincerely read the chapter. If they already know about the contents of the chapter they are suggested to undertake the *activities for auditors* for understanding the application of the contents in the chapter. Based on the difficulty level of activities the readers may refer to the matter presented in that chapter and others.

Each chapter also contains *figures* which describes the highlights and actions useful for academic. The experienced and learned readers can directly read the matter presented in the summary. If they find any comprehension difficulty they can read related matter further explained and also illustrated in figures as shown in certain places.

Formats are given towards the end of chapters to conduct the academic audit of relevant inputs, processes and outputs. In fact, formats help the auditors in following the provisions of academic audit holistically.

Activities for auditors given at the end of chapters are useful in applying the academic audit, mastering the theory of quality assurance and using it for quality management. It provides an opportunity for applying the learning of academic audit in real life situation. The readers are suggested to complete the activities after reading a particular chapter. The readers are suggested to interact on the output of completion of *activity for auditors* with their colleagues.

'Review questions' are given at the end of each chapter. These questions provide an opportunity to self-check the various dimensions of academic audit and quality management. These questions will certainly compel the readers to think and apply the learning outcomes of this book.

Towards the end of this book *Glossary of Terms* is given for a better understanding of the book. Glossary defines the major terms used in the book. Readers are suggested to refer to the glossary whenever they find a new term while reading a particular chapter.

Wish you all the best with a request to mail your valuable suggestions for improving the contents and presentation of the book. The readers are also requested to share their experiences and case studies.

1

Overview of Academic Audit

1. What is Academic Audit ?

The quality of products and services of the institution is achieved through scientifically designed academic systems (AS). The academic system comprises inputs, processes and outputs, and feedback to improve the quality of products and outputs. The inputs are fed to interactive processes to produce desired quality outputs. It means quality needs to be assured at every level, i.e. inputs, processes and outputs. The academic systems become the base for monitoring, sustaining, improving and innovating the quality.

Academic Audit (AA) is a recent concept came into existence in engineering colleges. *It is a systematic and scientific process of designing, implementing, monitoring and reviewing the quality of academic systems, i.e. inputs, processes and outputs.* It is a process of gathering information about current functioning of engineering colleges and comparing it with designed academic systems to draw conclusions about quality assurance of inputs, processes and outputs, i.e. products and services. It emphasises on reviewing the performance of the academic inputs, processes and outputs with respect to quality assurance. It emphasizes on core academic inputs, processes and outputs as well as supporting academic inputs, processes and outputs. It is not a fault finding, assessment and evaluation process but it is a system for assuring quality of products and services of the institution. It builds quality culture around the core academic processes of the institution. It helps institutions to align the quality efforts with the vision of the institution.

It is not the *review or assessment or academic monitoring or evaluation of the institution by statutory body against set national standards*. It is a scientific process in which wide variety of tools and techniques are used by the institution to design the academic systems, implement the systems and ultimately satisfy the requirements of the employers and stakeholders in effective and efficient manner. It emphasises on participative design of academic systems under the guidance of experts, install the systems, implement, monitor, review and improve them. The internal members of the institution are empowered to design, implement and improve the systems. They own the systems for self-satisfaction and satisfaction of the students, employers and stakeholders. It focuses on academic systems within the institution. It is different than financial audit in which the expenditures are audited with reference to rules. In AA the institute concentrates on assuring quality, improving quality and innovating new dimensions of quality. *The academic systems and AA contribute for maintenance, sustenance, improvement, value addition and innovation to achieve excellence in quality.* The journey for excellence in quality is illustrated in Fig. 1.1.

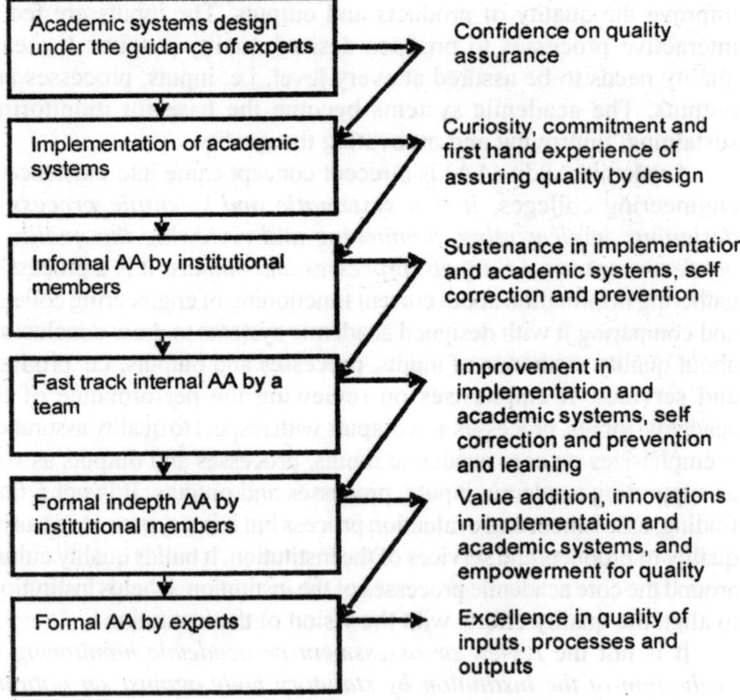

Fig. 1.1: Journey for Excellence in Quality

Fig. 1.1 illustrates that the institution should participatively design the AS under the guidance of team of experts. The involvement of institutional members in AS will educate them about the quality requirements and internalization of the quality systems. They will realize the importance of having AS in the institution. This approach is different than other approaches in which more emphasis is given on monitoring the quality without going into the details of the systems. The institution may satisfy the minimum quality requirements based on its experiences and traditional approach but it does not mean that the institution is observing quality systems. In such institutions the quality may get affected by any element, for example the trained and experienced faculty members retire or leave the job the quality will definitely come down. This is what happening with many institutions in the country.

On the contrary, such small changes will not affect the institutions having scientifically designed academic systems. The academic systems are the roots of quality initiatives so they will ensure spiral effect in the performance of the institution on quality parameters. The institutional members will be confident for implementation because they have quality systems in place. They will be encouraged to implement the systems and derive satisfaction out of it. The informal and formative AA will educate institutional members to improve the performance as well as systems.

The trained team of institutional members also conducts the AA to monitor the progress on quality in totality. It enables the institution to identify quality related problems as well as opportunities for value addition and innovations. The formal internal audit is conducted with the purpose to explore opportunities for improving and innovating the academic systems as a whole. The institutional members share the experiences of AS implementation, achievements and reflect on the same. They use the latest tools and techniques to refine the systems and their implementation mechanism.

AA *is a continuous process of design – validation – implementation–informal AA–refinement–implementation–fast track AA–improvement–implementation–indepth internal AA–innovation–implementation and excellence. It is a journey to accomplish quality excellence.*

2. What are the Purposes of Academic Audit ?

In general the AA serves numerous and variety of purposes for the institution and all the stakeholders of the institution. It is a proactive approach for assuring the quality of academic inputs, processes and outputs. It is a response to changing requirements of the world of work and students. The significant general purposes of academic audit are stated in Fig. 1.2.

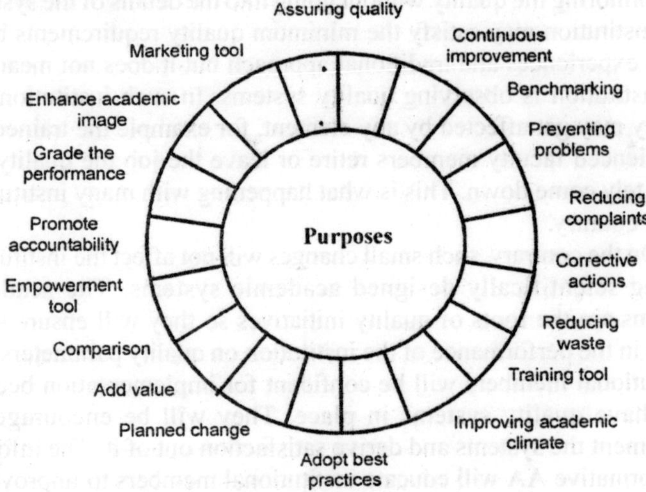

Fig. 1.2 : Purposes of Academic Audit

Assuring Quality

It is a quality assurance system of all academic inputs, possesses and outputs of the institution. The quality of output of academic products and services is ascertained through well-designed academic systems, processes and policies. Trained faculty and staff members implement the systems, processes and policies so there is less scope for adhoc and causal actions. The quality is assured at all stages and levels using direct and strong indicators of performance of the system.

Continuous Improvement

The AA is a tool for continuous improvement in the sense that it addresses at the roots of goals, inputs, processes, and actions. The quality of these elements is assured so that there is no scope for any chance of non-conformance to quality. The academic systems audit addresses the selection and design requirements of any of the elements among inputs and processes and improves the design after every AA. The improvement is judged through feedback and scientific inputs.

Benchmarking

The quality of inputs, processes and outputs is benchmarked for design and assurance purposes. The benchmarking is a very good tool to educate the institutional members about the minimum quality standards. The quality standards help the institution to spell out the expectations to internal and external stakeholders. The benchmarked performance inputs and outputs becomes the base for continuous improvement. The benchmarking is done with the best in the class and not with the national level minimum standards. The benchmarking may be governed by vision of the institution. For example the vision of the institution is *hundred per cent placement in national and multi-national companies*. Every input, process and output will be benchmarked with the vision of the institution.

Preventing Problems

The problems related to quantity are prevented through scientifically designed inputs, processes and outputs. For example the quality of inputs such as curriculum is assured through curriculum design process, competence of teachers is assured through their assessment and entry behaviour of students is assured through their entry behaviour test. Similarly the curriculum implementation problems are prevented and quality of learning is assured through course plan, competency plan, industrial training plan, laboratory/practical plan and lesson plan.

Reducing Complaints

At every stage the quality system is in place so the possibility related to complaints of the internal and external members is reduced. The approach of functioning of the institution shifts from reactive approach to proactive approach. The institution receives suggestions and innovative ideas from the internal and external stakeholders in contrast to complaints.

Corrective Actions

The institution has quality system in place so it is very easy to take corrective action. The points of corrective actions are easily located and actions can be immediately initiated at right time. The corrections made at right time provide immense level of satisfaction to the implementers of the curriculum.

Reducing Waste

The scientifically designed system of quality reduces the scope of wastage of time, money, and resources at every stage thereby improving the efficiency of functioning of the institution. It creates opportunities for joyful learning without any tension and stress.

Training Tool

Academic Audit is a tool of training for assuring quality at every phase of curriculum design, implementation and evaluation. The institutional members get ample opportunities for learning about quality during academic audit. They learn during academic audit system design, awareness and education workshops on AA, conducting and facing AA and implementing the recommendations of AA.

Improving Academic Climate

All the institutional members get involved at various phases of AA. They interact freely and frankly on issues related to assuring quality of graduates. They share problems, barriers and hurdles and jointly find the effective solutions to prevent the same in future. They come across innovations implemented by various faculty and staff members and learn from it. During this process the interpersonal relation and joint understanding of quality enhances. The commitment for quality increases. The participative approaches to quality assurance promote healthy academic climate in the institution.

Planned Change

It is said that quality can only be achieved by design and not by chance. The AA is a process of reviewing the quality systems of the institution in the light of their design and performance on assuring quality. It is a process of implementing planned changes in improving the performance of the institution. The academic audit provides constructive and positive feedback to improve the system.

Adopt Best Practices

The institution study the best practices being followed in centre of excellences and designs its system of quality. The institution also studies the academic audit system of the best in the class and adopt/adapt it. The faculty and staff members are provided ample opportunities to interact with institutions implementing academic systems and AA.

Add Value

The outcomes of formal and informal AA are used as feedback to assure the quality of performance of the academic system in next cycle. It adds value to quality assurance. The principle of design, assessment and educational technology are used for improving the process of audit of inputs, processes and outputs that is a kind of value addition.

Comparison

The comparison of academic system and performance is carried out to ensure effective implementation. The compression of inputs, processes and outputs of the institution and various departments within institution helps to locate and focus the improvement initiative.

Empowerment Tool

Numerous opportunities are available to institutional members for training, discussion and creativity on quality. They participate in design, monitoring, review and audit exercise. They get an opportunity to sharpen their skills on quality. They develop new abilities. They implement the academic systems and audit it; during this process they learn the tricks of the trade. The institution grants autonomy to its member to take quality related decisions and implement them.

Promote Accountability

The institution fixes responsibility for assuring quality at different stages and levels. The members are made accountable for quality through scientifically designed process. The involvement of the members in the academic audit system design and implementation enhances their self-accountability.

Grade the Performance

The performance of various inputs, processes and outputs are measured and graded for comparison. The measurement of performance of inputs helps to take decisions related to selection of inputs. Similarly the measurement of performance of outputs helps to take decisions about improving the quality of decisions.

Enhance Academic Image

The quality endeavours at each and every stage is publicized within and outside the institution. The quality of graduates and products becomes the source of publicity in world of work and society. The stakeholders get impressed from the quality of performance and academic innovations.

Marketing Tool

The academic system outcomes of AA are documented. The quality achievements endeavours are publicized to get more academic business from the employers and society for the growth and development of the institution.

The specific purposes of AA for various internal and external stakeholders are stated in Exhibit 1.1.

Exhibit 1.1 : Purposes of Academic Audit for Stakeholders

Stakeholders	*Purposes of AA*
Society	• The expectations of society are satisfied through academic audit reports. • The effective utilisation of public money is ensured in case of government institution.
Statutory body	• The maintenance of academic standards of the institution can be assured. • The quality of academic performance of different institutions can be compared. • Self-commitment for quality can be enforced on institutions. • The academic level of the institution can be publicized. • Best practices can be shared.
Employers	• Right types of graduates can be recruited. • Level of graduates and their salary can be decided. • Type of help and guidance to institutions can be decided. • The potential of the institution can be harnessed for various purposes such as continuing education, research and projects.

Exhibit 1.1 : *Contd.*

Stakeholders	*Purposes of AA*
	• Networking and collaborative projects can be undertaken.
Students	• Joyful learning. • Reduction of wastage of time, efforts and money. • Reduced tension and stress for learning. • Comparison on performance. • Healthy competition. • Career planning.
Parents	• Decision-making. • Help to institution. • Ascertaining level of quality of performance of institution.
Institution	• Using systematic and scientific processes. • Role clarity. • Enforcing accountability. • Training plans. • Estimating resources. • Marketing services. • Total quality management.
Teachers	• Clear roles and responsibility. • No wastage of time, efforts and money. • Effective documentation. • No confusion and conflict. • Empowerment.

3. What are the Characteristics of AA Process?

The AA should be designed to serve its intended purposes of quality assurance and improvement. The AA should have characteristics listed in Fig. 1.3.

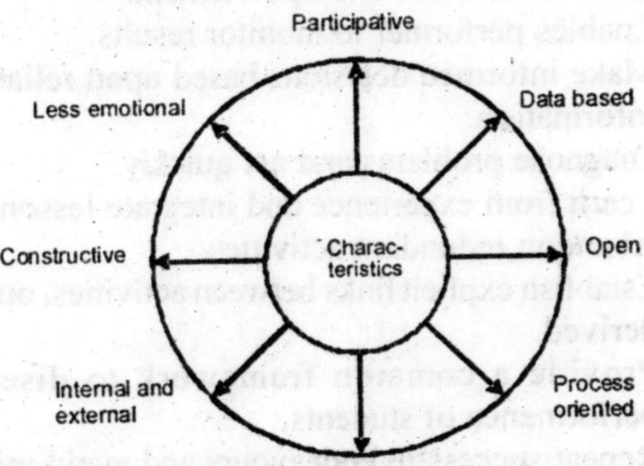

Fig. 1.3 : Characteristics of Academic Audit Process

3.1 Participative

Academic audit should be participative. All the interested persons should be involved in academic audit. In the language of total quality management internal as well as external customers should be involved in AA. The institutional members should be involved from the beginning of the quality and academic system design. Participation of institutional members from the beginning of the quality movement will enhance their commitment for implementing the system.

3.2 Data and Evidence Based

The AA should be conducted on the basis of factual data and performance standards set during the planning stage. The objectives are set for the semester or a year. In the process of objective setting all the significant stakeholders are involved. The institutional members prepare variety of plans to achieve different goals and objectives. One can take data from various plans prepared in different areas of functioning of the institute. The performance objectives should fulfil characteristics, such as clear, comprehensive, specific to the performance, measurable (quantitatively and qualitatively), deliverable, in tune with the institution objectives, challenging, attainable, development oriented and observable. The AA system should enable the individuals to produce benefits listed in Exhibit 1.2.

Exhibit 1.2 : Benefits at Auditor Level

1. Have an element of empowerment.
2. Enables performer to monitor results.
3. Make informed decisions based upon reliable performance information.
4. Diagnose problems and act quickly.
5. Learn from experience and integrate lessons learned.
6. Abandon redundant activities.
7. Establish explicit links between activities, outputs and results derived.
8. Provide a common framework to discuss quality of performance of students.
9. Repeat successful endeavours and avoid mistakes.
10. Share experiences and institutionalize it.

The AA is based on the principle, if we can measure performance, it can be manipulated. The quality of performance of teaching learning and other academic processes are recorded and records are produced during AA. It develops the habit of recording the data continuously in a systematic manner, which will provide continuous feedback regarding the progress of the work. This kind of documentation will be an evidence of progress.

3.3 Open System

The open system of AA not only prevents doubts and apprehensions about the quality but it also avoids the possibilities of bluffing, cheating and deceiving. People learn from good examples and mistakes of others. Open system helps to build up trust in interpersonal relationship. It provides an opportunity to exchange views on good practice of quality of performance.

3.4 Process Oriented

The AA should be carried out to measure the effectiveness and efficiency of the processes. It should focus core academic processes of the institution as stated in Exhibit 1.3. Depending on the objectives of the audit the breadth and depth of AA may be decided by audit team.

3.5 Value Addition

In every cycle it enhances the effectiveness and efficiency of processes. It makes the quality standards more stringent but at the same time achievable. In educational institutions the AA promotes joy, fun, interest, and humour. It adds value in academic processes as well as products.

3.6 Internal and External

Internal as well external members conduct audit with a purpose. Initially, the experts participatively design the academic systems and guide implementation of it. Gradually internal members conduct the academic audit and bring improvement in the system. The members of the institution get variety of feedback from the auditors and learn to enhance the quality of processes. They receive feedback to improve their performance through training and development activities. Over the years, all institutional members get involved in AA activities of the institution. It is a very powerful method of installing quality system in the institution and obtaining quality certificate.

3.7 Constructive

The AA is introduced in the institution for enhancing the capability and capacity in delivering the goods and services. The introduction of AA is possible when it is constructive and focuses on improvement of the performance of the students. It is not considered fault-finding process but a process to promote mutual trust, appreciation and development for the quality of learning.

3.8 Less Emotional

The system of AA, based on facts and data, is helpful in providing constructive feedback to process designers and performers. It avoids the chances of incorporation of emotional parameters such as very old employee, performed very well during the crisis time, honest person, relatives of influential person, never oppose the decisions of management, traditional process and so on.

4. What are the Types of Academic Audit?

The AA can be classified on various criteria in different ways. The criteria and classification of academic audit is shown in Fig. 1.4.

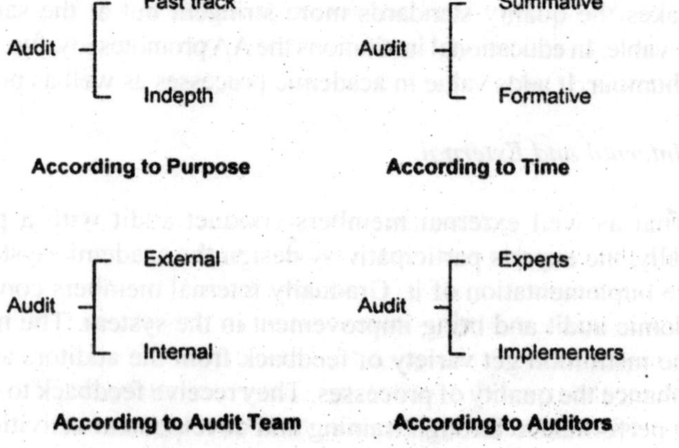

Fig. 1.4 : Types of Academic Audit

Fast Track and Indepth Academic Audit

Fast Track AA : The fast track AA is conducted on significant inputs, processes and outputs on significant and direct parameters to quickly know the status of the institutional performance or any educational programme. In fast track AA quantitative as well as qualitative parameters are considered for audit. It superficially reveals the quantitative as well as qualitative performance of the institution or a particular programme. The governing body or the management of the institution takes significant policy decisions on quality system of the institution. It is generally conducted by experts and outside persons to prevent the biases in conducting audit and arriving at results. It is a sample and random audit of inputs, processes and outputs. The fast track AA is conducted on overall performance of the institution on all the parameters of inputs, processes and outputs. The audit is conducted on randomly selected samples and on broad criteria. This audit is conducted to assess the quality of performance of the quality system as a whole. It provides the information for policy decisions and solve academic systems problem. The duration of audit is kept very short say one day. It is conducted after implementation of one cycle of the system.

Indepth AA: On the other hand indepth AA is conducted by the teaching and non-teaching staff preferably under the guidance of the experts. It is conducted on all the inputs, process and outputs for improving the performance of academic systems on quality parameters and core processes. It is conducted by the person responsible for implementing the core processes and peers to provide and receive feedback on quality of performance. This is considered an educative exercise for one and all in the institution to assure quality, add value, improve performance, review process and take corrective and preventive actions.

Summative and Formative Academic Audit

Summative AA : The summative AA is conducted by a team of internal as well as external experts drawn from various fields such as core discipline, education management, education technology, curriculum development, assessment and the like. The frequency of summative AA is decided based on numerous factors such as programmes offered by the institution, competition faced by institution, challenges ahead, demand for quality, time and money available for audit purposes and the like. The summative AA assures the quality of performance of systems for next cycle of implementation of the programmes say four years. It is a holistic approach to assure and improve the quality of performance of the institution. Generally, the summative AA is conducted every fifth year. The institution takes significant decisions on quality systems of the institution on the basis of the results of the summative AA. The major decisions such as re-engineering the curriculum, recruitment of teachers, infrastructure development, admission policy, development of instructional resources and the like are taken on the basis of summative AA.

Formative AA: The formative AA is a continuous process conducted by institutional members for assuring the quality of performance of day to day processes such as effectiveness of instructional methods, practical, industrial training, project work, assignments etc. It is a learning exercise for all the members. The institution provides opportunity to its members for sharing the academic audit experiences in the form of meetings, workshops, seminars, feedback sessions and conferences. The members learn through sharing their experiences to improve quality of performance. In most of the cases it is an informal method of conducting the audit. The inputs, processes and outputs are refined, modified and adjusted on the basis of formative AA. It may be formally conducted every semester and informally conducted after every significant learning event, say after completion of every unit in a particular course.

External and Internal Academic Audit

External AA : A team of experts conducts it to identify the strengths and weaknesses of the academic systems and suggest improvement measures. At the same time it shares the best practices being implemented in various institutions with the faculty and staff members of the institution. It makes recommendations to modify the current academic system, design new system using information and educational technology and implement best practices. It influences the governing body and members of the institution to bring improvements in the academic systems.

Internal AA: It is a process of auditing the performance of the academic systems by the internal members of the institution. It is a process of enhancing the accountability and commitment of the institutional members for implementing quality systems in totality and spirit. It develops the collective understanding of institutional members about the quality systems and their benefits. All the institutional members are trained to conduct the internal AA with reference to its objectives. It prevents confusion and conflict among the members. It also prevents deviation in conducting the audit and ensures effective communication.

The internal AA is conducted observing the code of conduct/norms for conducting the audit. It is a formal audit conducted after completion of every semester. It is a sort of formative academic audit that emphasizes on observing the performance of academic system. It points out the non-conformance to the systems and reasons thereof. It is a learning and improvement exercise for one and all in the institution. It also tests the effectiveness, relevance, efficiency, practicability and alignment of the academic systems with the institutions goals and missions, if the systems are designed and implemented for the first time. The internal audit reveals the functional problems of the system at the same time specific methodology that works.

Experts and Internal

Audit conducted by Experts: As described earlier experts are involved in designing the academic systems to assure quality, effectiveness and efficiency. The experts provide inputs from various dimensions of the quality to the design of the systems. They make aware and educate institutional members about importance of having academic systems. They guide the institution to implement the academic system and enjoy quality. They are also involved in AA process after one cycle of implementation of the educational programmes say after five years. The AA conducted by experts reveals the system gaps. They provide latest inputs to academic systems design.

Audit conducted by Internal Members: As described earlier the internal members are involved in the complete process of AS design right from the beginning. They internalise the intent of the academic systems and their significance. It is the essential feature of AA because no external experts can assure quality of implementation of AS. The internal AA is purely diagnostic and formative. It is informal when implementers use it consciously to review the performance and take corrective or value addition initiatives on their own. It is also formally conducted with a purpose at the end of the semester. The internal members are involved in performing and observing the provisions of the systems as well as auditing the systems and performance. The internal audit brings variety of and numerous benefits to the institution. The significant benefits are : refinement and perfection of competencies of all the members, continuous improvement in performance, corrective action at right time without intervention of management or external experts, sense of achievement and satisfaction, positive and constructive feedback, greater ownership for quality, building quality culture and enjoyment of fruits of quality. The parameters of inputs, processes and outputs are stated in Exhibit 1.3.

Exhibit 1.3 : Parameters of Fast Track Academic Audit

Inputs

Entry behaviour of students	Existences of process of measuring their aptitude, attitude, ambition, aspiration and capability to pursue the study
Curriculum	Existence of scientifically designed curriculum development/selection process
Faculty and staff	Existence of scientifically designed recruitment process based on core competency of the faculty and staff
Learning resources	Existence of scientifically designed learning resources development/selection processes

Processes

Curriculum implementation plans	Existence of scientifically designed teaching learning strategy
Course plan	Existence of scientifically designed process of preparing course plan and criteria of evaluation
Competency plan	Existence of scientifically designed process of preparing competency plan and criteria of evaluation
Lesson plan	Existence of scientifically designed process of preparing lesson plan and criteria of evaluation
Laboratory experiments	Existence of scientifically designed process of conducting laboratory experiments and criteria of evaluation
Industrial training	Existence of scientifically designed process of organising industrial training and criteria of evaluation
Certification of competency/ assessment	Existence of scientifically designed process of assessing learning and certifying competency and criteria of certification/assessment
Performance	Existence of scientifically designed process of assessing performance of teaching and non-teaching staff and criteria of appraisal

Exhibit 1.3 : *Contd.*

Outputs

Certification of competencies and award of degree	Existence of scientifically designed process of certifying competencies for award of degree and criteria of certification
Curriculum revision	Existence of scientifically designed process of curriculum evaluation and revision
Training and development of faculty and staff	Existence of scientifically designed process of training and development of faculty and staff
Learning resources	Existence of scientifically designed processes of learning resources development/revision/selection

5. How AA is Different than Accreditation and Evaluation?

The AA is different than other contemporary concepts of managing quality of education. The contemporary concepts are explained on various criteria stated in Exhibit 1.4.

Exhibit 1.4 : Contemporary Concept of Quality Management and AA

Criteria	*Academic audit*	*Accreditation*	*Evaluation*
Concept	Review of inputs, processes and outputs with AS for quality	Overall assessment of institution & programme against national norms	Review of the performance of the institution against goals.
Purpose	Assure quality of performance	Recognition for minimum level of quality	Ascertain level of performance against institutional goals
Frequency	Internal yearly and External every five years	Every three or five years	According to needs
Bench-marking	Possible with the best in the class and within the institution	Possible with the minimum level at national level	Not possible
Aligned to vision	Yes, every input, process and output is aligned to vision by design	Not necessary, depends on statutory body criteria	Yes
Value addition	At the root level	Uncertain	Ad hoc and causal
Performance	Assuring performance	Performance against standards	Performance against goals

6. What are the Assumptions for Conducting AA?

The Academic Audit can be designed and implemented for any educational institution and it will result in better quality of academic performance of the institution as well as individuals. The AA brings best and immediate results in those institutions that fulfil the requirements of assumptions as stated in Fig. 1.5. These assumptions are described briefly in subsequent paragraphs.

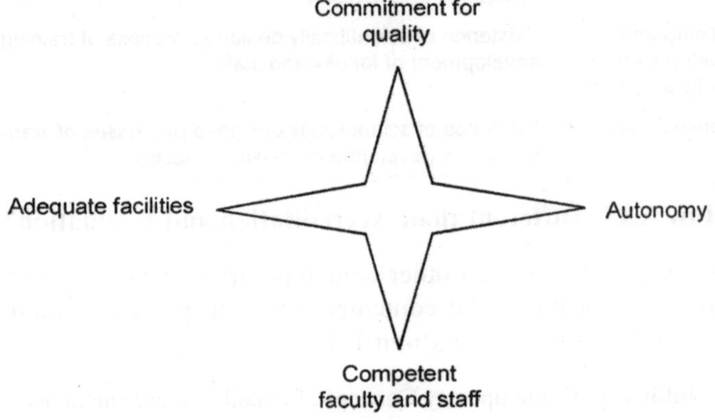

Fig. 1.5 : Assumptions for Academic Audit

Commitment for Quality

The governing body, management of the institution, faculty members, staff members and students are committed for quality of learning that satisfies needs of the employers and society. It is assumed that the institute has quality policy, quality processes and rewards for quality in place. The faculty and staff are dedicated for quality of learning. They believe in practicing scientifically designed quality processes. The institution management and its faculty members do not compromise with quality standards for immediate gain. The faculty and students are self-motivated to learn and develop on their own. The institutional members are involved in quest for quality. If this assumption is valid the institution can do miracle on competence and professionalism of the graduates. It will feed the graduates to industry who are ready to accept the challenges of the world of work. If the institution is not having quality systems in place the introduction of AA may be an instrument to educate the governors, educational managers and faculty members to systematize the things. It will not give immediate significant results. The fruits of academic audit are varied and many. It all depends on the level of institutional functioning on quality parameters.

Autonomy

Academic Audit is beneficial in institutions where the autonomy has percolated down the line. Teachers and students enjoy autonomy to take decisions related to selection of courses, time, teaching learning method, mode and method of assessment with a strong determination to develop competency and proficiency. The students are empowered to learn scientifically without tension and stress. There is no curriculum provision for following a rigid path with compulsion. Now the time has come where the discipline barriers should be removed and total flexibility should be provided to students to learn.

Competent Faculty and Staff

The faculty and staff members are competent to offer the courses desired by students. They are capable to satisfy the changing requirements of the students and industry. They get an opportunity to work and feel the corporate culture. They are generously sponsored for training in emerging and new areas. At the same time they are trained to transfer learning to students up to predefined level. They are encouraged to conduct researches and experiments to enhance the quality, efficiency and effectiveness of learning.

Adequate Facilities

The institution has adequate facilities in terms of men, material, machine, money, minutes and information to perform the activities. The institutional members are having healthy relationship among themselves and with the students. The institution has network and collaboration with centre of excellences and resource centres. The values and norms of the institution promote motivational culture and climate. The institution provides right kinds of inputs at right time for carrying out the activities. The teamwork, creativity, innovation, development and value addition in performance is encouraged and appreciated by one and all.

7. What is AA Cycle?

There are five major phases for managing AA in the institution. The auditors and auditees professionally carry out these phases. They learn to increase the effectiveness and efficiency of audit process at the same time they come across weakness of audit system. The learning of auditors and auditees bring continuous improvement in the performance of the institution. The AA cycle is shown in Fig. 1.6.

Fig. 1.6 : Academic Audit Cycle

8. How AAS is Developed?

The AAS is developed for inputs, processes, and outputs that are the elements of vision and mission reach strategies. The AS is designed along with the institutional strategic plan as stated in Fig. 1.7.

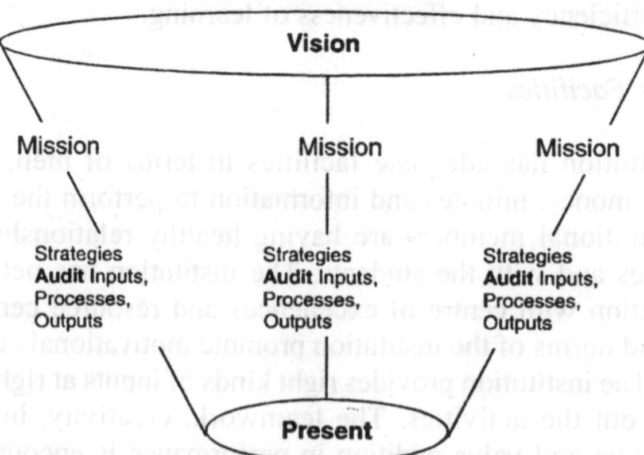

Fig. 1.7 : Integrated Academic Audit System

The AS is designed along with the strategic plan of the institution. A team of experts involving all significant members of the institution designs the AS. It is generally designed through series of workshops conducted by a team of experts.

Awareness Workshop

The team conducts short duration (4–8 hours) workshops to create awareness about AA among the faculty and staff members. In this workshop they discuss the concept, purpose, benefits, broad approach of conducting the AA, role and responsibilities of faculty and staff members and the like. After this workshop a week time is provided to institutional members to seriously think on the philosophy of AA. They are provided relevant literature containing case studies, anecdote, and interviews of eminent persons having authority on AA. They study the literature and reflect on it with their colleagues. The institutional members are given assignments in small groups to think and come out with feasible solutions, strategies and ideas on assignment. The indicative assignments are stated in Exhibit 1.5.

Exhibit 1.5 : Assignments for Institutional Members

1. Are we really following AS in our institutions?
2. What are the gaps in current AS?
3. We are already accredited by National Board of Accreditation (NBA) or National Assessment and Accreditation Council (NAAC) should we go for AA?
4. What should be the scope of AA in our institution?
5. What are the core academic systems?
6. How should we design the core academic systems?
7. How should we implement the core academic systems?
8. Who should conduct the internal AA?
9. Will the AA increase unnecessary workload on faculty and staff members?
10. Will Governing Board and management of institution support and sustain AA?
11. Will the institutional members get personal benefit out of implementing AA?
12. Will the students and significant stakeholders get benefit from AA?

13. Which policy initiatives are required to install AA?
14. If AA is implemented, how will it facilitate obtaining other quality certificates?

Education and Motivation Workshop

The institutional members ponder upon the assignments and come out with solutions, strategies and ideas. The next workshop is organised to educate and motivate the institutional members to go for AA. In this workshop they are provided an opportunity to make presentation or discuss the outcomes of the assignments. They also discuss the significant issues raised during discussion and decide to go for AA. The resistance to change is removed satisfying the queries of the faculty and staff members and taking appropriate actions for mobilizing the resources for assuring the quality. During the workshops all the issues related to quality of products and services are addressed. The experts, higher management members and institutional members identify the core academic inputs, processes and outputs. They chart the current practices related to academic inputs, processes and outputs. They identify the gaps, weaknesses and deficiencies in the academic inputs, processes and outputs with respect to current practices and future requirements.

AS Design Workshop

The education and motivation workshop create adequate interest in institutional members to reengineer the current AS or redesign it. Based on the gaps and deficiencies, they identify the new inputs, processes and outputs and design them to assure quality at every stage and level of performance.

Inputs Audit Design

The audit of institutional plan is carried out first so the institutional plans are designed for assuring quality at institutional level. The institutional vision, strategic plan, perspective plan and annual plan are audited before going for academic details of programmes and courses. The audit of vision, strategic plan, perspective plan and annual plan is conducted on quality and process of crafting them as stated in Exhibit 1.6.

Exhibit 1.6 : Audit of Institutional Development Plans

Item	*Process of*	*Characteristics of*
Vision	Crafting	Vision
Strategic plan	Preparing	Plan
Perspective plan	Preparing	Plan
Annual plan	Preparing	Plan

The audit for inputs and process of selection of inputs is carried out on the parameters stated in Exhibit 1.7. The quality of inputs is assessed on quality of design of processes and criteria used for selection of inputs. The process and criteria are updated after every internal AA cycle (one year) to continually improve the quality of inputs.

Exhibit 1.7 : Audit of Inputs

Inputs	*Process of selection*	*Criteria*
Curriculum	Curriculum development process (Refer format)	Quality of curriculum
Students	Admission process (Refer format)	Quality of students – Profile – percentage, preferences, hobbies, aspirations,
Teachers	Recruitment process (Refer format)	Quality of teachers – Profile- competencies, Qualification, Experience, Training, Achievements,
Learning resources Selection	Learning resources selection process	Criteria
Students assessment	Evaluation, Evaluation method, frequency, decisions for revision	Criteria for evaluation
Infrastructure	Development process	Criteria for quality of infrastructure

Processes Audit Design

The processes are designed scientifically using principles of education psychology, education technology, andragogy, curriculum design, education management, and information technology. These processes are designed to produce the desired quality of end products (development of competencies in students) and services. The AA is designed for all, processes whether they are core or supporting. The outputs of some intermediate processes may be input to subsequent process. The processes are designed considering following questions:

- What is process?
- Where does it start and end?
- Who is the beneficiary of the process?
- What are the requirements to implement the process?
- How well are they met?
- What are improvement goals?
- What are the activities and flow?
- Do they all add value to learning process?
- Can they be done more quickly?
- Is there a radical alternative?

The audit is conducted for core processes if it is fast track audit. The AA of all processes is carried out if it is indepth. The significant processes and audit parameters are stated in Exhibit 1.8.

Exhibit 1.8 : Audit of Processes

Significant processes design	Effectiveness and efficiency of process
Training and development process of faculty and staff members	Criteria
Implementation of curriculum	**Effectiveness of process**
Teaching learning methods	Criteria for planning implementation, evaluation and improvement of the process based on the feedback
Lecture	
Role play	
Group discussion	
Case method	
Buzz group	
Presentations	
Question answer	
Creativity sessions	
In-basket	
Assignments – home, computer, industrial, library, internet	
Laboratory experiments	
Industrial training	
Projects	
Seminars/conferences/symposium	
Competition/game	
Simulation	
Workshop practice	

Exhibit 1.8 : *Contd.*

Panel discussions	
Development and use of learning resources	Criteria
Print (Handouts, notes, case studies etc.)	
Non-print (Overhead projector transparencies, video films, power point presentations, etc.)	
Evaluation of resources	Criteria
Organising resources	Criteria
Assessment of learning of students	
• Formative	
• Summative	
Co-curricular activities	
• Guidance and counselling	Criteria
• Awareness	
• Sports	
• Personality development	
• Hobby development	
• Games	
• Quiz, etc.	

Output Audit Design

The outputs are designed according to the needs of the employers and stakeholders. The graduates should satisfy the needs of emerging challenges and competition in the world of work. The outputs are audited on stringent criteria derived from quality requirements. The criteria for auditing the outputs are stated in Exhibit 1.9.

Exhibit 1.9 : Quality of Output

Outputs	*Process*	*Criteria for measuring quality*
Students	Exit test	Honours, first division, second division, certification of core competencies, certification of peripheral competencies, certification of professional competencies.
Teachers	Performance appraisal	Achievements (qualitative and quantitative), experiences and expertise developed
Learning resources used by the teacher	Audit	Innovative, effective, efficient, relevant resources

Exhibit 1.9 : *Contd.*

Outputs	*Process*	*Criteria for measuring quality*
Researches	Audit	Uniqueness, patents, revenue earned, name earned
Continuing education programmes	Audit	Qualitative and quantitative achievements, revenue earned, material developed, linkages developed
Evaluation of curriculum	Research based approach	Relevance, acceptance, higher placement, more demand, appreciations, consultancy or guidance sought by other institutions, additional competencies developed

All the institutional members and experts should validate the audit formats. The formats are tried out for relevance, practicability and feasibility and further refined. The formats for auditing the inputs, processes and outputs are numbered and documented in the AA manual. The implementation of system is carried out using academic system to do *the right things first time and every time*. The audit is conducted using these formats by internal and external audit teams.

All the institutional members are educated to use the academic systems effectively and efficiently. They are provided necessary resources to implement the academic systems. They are also trained to do the informal and internal audit and refine their skills to assure quality. They are trained to maintain the records of achievements and produce them as evidence during internal and external audit.

9. How AA is Conducted?

The institution should prepare the AA plan addressing the objectives and activities of the AA with respect to time. The institutional members involved in implementing the academic processes conduct the audit. This will enable them to take first hand feedback on the performance of the processes and quality of output. They will come to know the weaknesses and strengths of processes. They will reflect on performance of the processes and learn to refine them for improving the effectiveness and efficiency of the processes in next cycle of the audit. The academic audit plan is prepared considering the purposes of the AA and other significant operational factors.

A team constituted for the purposes of AA also undertakes the audit exercise and finds out the effectiveness and efficiency of the academic processes. It examines the performance of all the significant and core academic processes of the institution and takes decisions to modify, refine and add value to the processes for the next cycle. The team approach provides better insight to the inputs, processes and outputs. It helps to simplify everything. It also analyses the implementation problems of academic systems.

Generally academic audit week is organised after every semester/ year to conduct the informal audit. The teachers and other process owners keep all the implementation records ready for self–audit and internal team audit. They exhibit favourable behaviour for the AA because it is not an evaluation process but quality assurance process.

The Academic Audit Manual (AAM) is used for conducting the AA. The audit team and the institutional members follow the audit norms. The indicative AA norms are stated in Exhibit 1.10.

Exhibit 1.10 : AA Norms for Auditors

1. Use people's skills and create conducive environment for AA.
2. Effectively communicate the purpose of AA.
3. Ask for the preparation made by auditees for the audit.
4. See the documents and other evidences prepared by auditees for implementing quality systems.
5. Record the facts, figures and data.
6. Record quantitative as well as qualitative achievements.
7. Be punctual, fair, objective, honest and sincere during the process of audit.
8. Maintain confidentiality of information and documents wherever necessary.
9. Record problems faced by implementers.
10. Provide adequate opportunities to auditees to share their feelings about academic systems and their experiences.
11. Do not criticize the auditees for non-achievement of objectives or quality.
12. Appreciate the efforts and problems of the people. Ask about the solution of the problem they are facing. If asked, provide constructive suggestions.
13. Everyone is putting efforts for quality so promote mutual help.

Contd.

Exhibit 1.10 : ***Contd.***

14. Do not impose your views on members.
15. Discuss the normal things and leave the extreme events.
16. Note the suggestions of auditees for improving the system.
17. Thank the auditees for their cooperation.

The format of preparing internal academic audit plan is shown in Exhibit 1.11.

Exhibit 1.11 : Format for AA Plan

Objectives of the internal academic audit:

Scope of the internal audit :

Activities	*Duration*	*Responsibility*	*Auditee's activities*
Formation of internal audit teams and term of reference	1 week	Director of the institution	Team clarifies its role and allocates responsibility to its members
Information to departments and individuals about the academic audit and preparation according to audit manual	1 week	Audit team	Clarification, if any
Preparation and self audit by performers	1 week	Departments	Preparation and self audit
Department-wise presentation by performers on adherence to quality system, problems faced, improvement measures, value addition and opportunities for further improvement	1 week	Departments and audit team	Presentation
Department-wise report preparation by internal auditors	1 week	Audit team	
Compilation of reports at institution level	1 week	Audit team	
One day seminar on outputs of AA and quality	One day	Audit team and experts	
Implementation of significant decisions in next cycle	One year	All institutional members	Following decisions based on AA

The duration mentioned in duration column is indicative time provided to the individuals. It does not mean that institutional members will devote so much time for that particular activity. The institution should entertain external audit team or accreditation team visit or ISO team visit after design, implementation and internal audit of academic systems of the institution. It is a base for all types of audit, accreditation, assessment, evaluations and innovations.

10. What should be the Code of Conduct of Auditees?

The AA is conducted for bringing improvement and value addition in the quality of products and services of the institution and not for evaluating the performance of the institutional members. It is a learning exercise about quality systems for one and all in the institution. Everyone should fully cooperate and facilitate the process of AA in the institution. The institutional members should create conducive environment for internal as well as external AA. The institutional members should observe the norms stated in Exhibit 1.12.

Exhibit 1.12 : AA Norms for Auditees

1. Carry out documentation of performance as mentioned in the AA manual.
2. Listen the questions of auditors and then respond.
3. Show them evidences and documents to support your answer.
4. Welcome the suggestions of auditors for implementing the systems and improving the performance.
5. Do not try to impress the auditors using influencing strategies.
6. Be proactive and positive during the audit process.
7. Demonstrate commitment to audit process and auditor.

11. Which Tools and Techniques are used for Designing AS and Conducting AA?

The process of AA starts with design of academic systems in the light of vision, mission and goals of the institution. In the design of academic systems various tools such as process design flow charts, problem analysis tree and plans are used. The institutional members use techniques such as interactions, meetings, workshops, presentations, creativity sessions and the like. The team members use principles of education technology, education psychology, information technology, and education management for designing the academic systems. The academic audit is conducted using various tools and techniques. The tools are designed using various significant and direct criteria for auditing the quality of inputs, processes and outputs. These tools and techniques are designed and prescribed in the academic audit manual. Generally' the formats in the form of rating scale is used to audit the quality of inputs, rating scale and observation schedule are used to audit the processes and rating scale is used to audit the quality of outputs. Audit team uses the presentation, interview, observation, interaction and record analysis techniques during audit process. The indicative formats for auditing the academic systems are given in subsequent Chapters and appended as Appendix I at the end of this book.

12. What should be the Frequency of Academic Audit?

Generally, the audit frequency is kept six months to a year because the impact of inputs, processes and outputs can be seen after completion of one cycle. If the audit is conducted for curriculum development process its frequency may be one year. If the audit is conducted for a use of specific teaching learning method its frequency may be a semester. The type of AA and frequency is stated in Exhibit 1.13.

Exhibit 1.13 : AA and Frequency

Audit	*Fast track*	*Indepth*
Formative	After completion of every significant learning event or competency (implementers self audit)	After every year (internal audit)
Summative	Every semester (internal audit)	Every fifth year (external audit)

13. How much time should be devoted for conducting the Internal and External AA?

The institution should plan the internal or external AA during the lean period or during vacation. The academic audit should be finished in three to five days. It does not mean that everyone will be busy in conducting the AA for three to five days. The AA team may be involved for three to five days and individuals will be involved for 5 to 8 hours in a period of three to five days. If the self-audit, informal audit and internal audit is the culture of the institution the formal AA is considered to be a normal activity. If it is not the part of functioning of the institution it takes more time for preparation, arranging and organising the things in order.

14. Who should conduct the AA?

At different levels and for different purposes different persons conduct the AA. In fact the concept of 360-degree audit should be used for conducting the academic audit. The auditors for 360-degree audit are stated in Fig. 1.8.

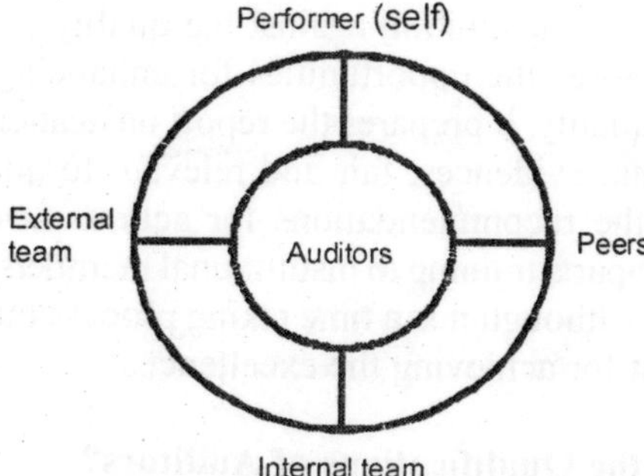

Fig. 1.8 : 360 Degree Audit – Auditors

Audit by Performer (Self)

The performers are encouraged to conduct the self-audit consciously and reflect on the results of the same. The self-audit refines the skills of the performers to assure quality. It is a process to enhance commitment, thinking and satisfaction of the performers.

Peers

The peers are involved in the audit process to develop audit skills and share quality related experiences and problems. They generate the feasible solution to the common problems. They reflect on the performance of the AS and if necessary refine it to remove bottlenecks of performance and quality. It creates mutual accountability of institutional members for assuring quality. It creates a kind of social pressure on each other to implement the quality systems.

Internal Team

The internal team conducts yearly sample AA to diagnose quality related problems at institutional level. It generates solutions to common problems and recommends the management and institutional members to implement the solutions. It also explores the opportunity for value addition in quality of products and services.

External Team

The external team conducts the indepth audit of quality systems and performance of the institution against the quality policy and quality systems. It explores the opportunities for enhancing and expanding parameters of quality. It prepares the report on academic audit, which is based on data, evidences, fair and relevant to quality. The report clearly spells the recommendations for actions at all levels in the institution. It imparts training to institutional members to refine quality related efforts. Although it is a time taking process but the institutions should go for it for achieving the excellence.

15. What are the Qualifications of Auditors?

All the internal as well as external auditors should be trained to acquire competencies to design, implement, and conduct AA of the institution. Experts train them so that they can perform the role effectively and efficiently in the light of scope and purpose of AA. They are trained to acquire the competencies stated in Exhibit 1.14.

Exhibit 1.14 : Competencies of Auditors

Essential Competencies

1. Design AS for higher and technical institutions.
2. Use of tools and techniques in academic AS.
3. Implement quality systems in the institution.
4. Use principles of continuous improvement and value addition in implementation.
5. Modify/refine system to prevent quality problems.
6. Take corrective actions.
7. Prepare audit plan.
8. Conduct discussions, interviews, private meetings and workshops for AA.

Contd.

Exhibit 1.14 : *Contd.*

9. Systematically document the information and observation.
10. Draw conclusions and write recommendations on the basis of facts, figures and observation.
11. Prepare audit report.
12. Present audit conclusions and recommendations to institutional members.

Desirable Competencies

1. Communicate effectively on various issues of AA.
2. Observe the quality culture in the functioning of the institution.
3. Be supportive to auditees during the audit process.
4. Impart training on quality related issues to institutional members.

Professional Competencies

1. Show concern about quality of products, processes and inputs.
2. Appreciate quality initiatives undertaken by institute.
3. Explore opportunities for enhancing quality of systems.

16. Which Documents are to be maintained for AA?

The institution maintains variety of documents for undergoing external AA of the institution. The proper maintenance of hard and soft copy facilitates the process of conduction of external AA. The institution maintains documents stated in Exhibit 1.15.

Exhibit 1.15 : Documents of External AA

1. Academic systems
2. AA manual developed participatively under the guidance of experts
3. All reports of internal AA
4. Actions taken on the basis of internal AA
5. Strategic plan of the institution
6. Achievements (quantitative as well as qualitative) of the institution
7. All significant evidences in various forms

The institutional members are also encouraged to maintain the documents and evidences that can be shared during the internal AA. The institutional members can maintain the documents stated in Exhibit 1.16.

Exhibit 1.16 : Documents for Internal AA

1. Curriculum document
2. Course/subject plan
3. Lesson plan
4. Laboratory plan
5. Industrial training plan and report
6. Learning resources
7. Outputs of assignments
8. Laboratory manual of students
9. Outputs of seminars, conferences and symposium
10. Real life problem solving
11. Research studies
12. Report of industrial projects
13. Report of industrial training
14. Diary
15. Attendance record
16. Self-development activities undertaken
17. Report of continuing education programmes

17. What should be the Format of AA Report?

The AA report is key to significant decision-making process for improving the performance of the institution. The report should reflect the true picture of quality systems and their implementation. It should not criticize a person but focus on inputs, processes and outputs. The AA report is a public document and is used by internal and external stakeholders so it should not communicate the wrong message to any stakeholder. The report should be precise, fair, clear, communicable and objective. Competent authority should release the AA report after verifying it. If it is a report prepared by external team it should be validated by the competent authority before release. The report should raise the significant issues, problems and barriers related to quality. It should also highlight the best practices and their impact on the quality of performance. The recommendations should be significant, important, and applicable to the whole quality system. It should not unnecessariiy drag trivial quality issues in a big way. The recommendation should emphasise fresh approach to quality if it is external audit conducted by experts. The report should also point out the gap between internal audit and external audit. The format of the AA report depends on scope and objectives of the audit. However, the format for reporting internal and external AA results is described in Exhibit 1.17.

Exhibit 1.17 : Format for Internal AA Report

Chapter 1 : About the Institution—Describes the history of the institution/department, vision, missions, quality policy of the institution and its distinct features.

Chapter 2 : About the AA—Describes the scope, purposes, academic inputs, processes and outputs as stated in AAM and its adherence with the same. The major quantitative and qualitative achievements and deviations from quality systems, problems faced in implementing quality systems and solutions thereof.

Chapter 3 : Conclusions and Recommendations—Describes the recommendations on; improving the systems design, refining the policy, providing the resources, enhancing the capability of the institutional members and preventing the problems in future. The audit team recommends value addition measures to assure and improve quality at institution level. The quality initiatives and efforts are appreciated in the report. The best practices are recorded and acknowledged for wider use.

Appendix : List of significant evidences is appended.

18. What should be the Impact of AA on Performance of the Institution?

The journey of quality starts from academic systems. The academic systems are the foundation rock for assuring and improving quality of performance. It is the initiative point for all the innovations in functioning of the institution. The AA has short-term as well as long-term impact on the performance and corporate image of the institution. The outcomes of AA depend on the duration for which it is practiced. If it is sincerely, honestly and scientifically practiced for four years, it has long-term impact on the academic image of the institution. If it is practiced for short term it will improve efficiency of functioning of the institution. The parameters to measure impact of the academic audit are stated in Fig. 1.9.

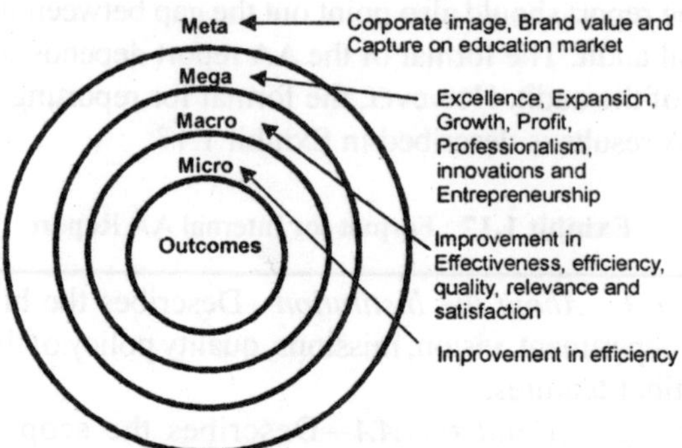

Fig. 1.9 : Outcomes of Academic Audit

The AA brings immediate improvement in the performance of the individuals and institution because it saves time and efforts of faculty and support staff. The scientifically designed systems are implemented and audited informally so it enhances effectiveness, efficiency, relevance and quality in one semester. If the academic systems are implemented for a year with informal and internal audit it improves effectiveness, efficiency, relevance and quality of programmes. It provides immense level of satisfaction to institutional members and students because they have different experience than traditional. The instructional processes create joy in learning experiences. Students get ample hands on learning opportunities in the campus and outside the campus. They learn in close to real life situation. Their interest, ambition, aspiration and curiosity for learning are ignited. It is the case with faculty members and teaching staff, they get an opportunity to do something systematically and scientifically. They also learn new professional skills and refine previously developed skills.

The institution functions professionally and learns from formal and informal internal audit. It gets publicity for quality and innovations. The students and stakeholders demand for services. It starts new and innovative projects to satisfy the demands of students and stakeholders. The growth and development becomes the integral part of the plans of the institution. Faculty and staff members are encouraged to do experimentation for improving the design of the systems and their implementation.

Over a period of four years the institution builds up corporate image for quality and innovations. It is known for unique quality of graduates, services and products. The students, industry and stakeholders function collaboratively with the institution for mutual benefits. The institution captures the market of education and training.

19. How the Recommendations of AA are used for improving the Quality of Academic Systems and Performance?

The general recommendations made in external AA report are used for refining the policies, guidelines, academic systems, implementation processes and internal audit processes. These recommendations are implemented by one and all to prevent quality problems, take corrective actions and bring improvement in performance. The corrective actions are first taken at input level then process level and then output level. The institutional members try to treat the root cause of the problem so that problems do not recur. For example if there is a problem with design of the curriculum the curriculum is scientifically designed and then implemented. If there is a problem related to ability of the faculty members they are trained and then they are asked to perform the specific role. The general recommendations are learning and implementation points for one and all in the institution. Management of the institution seriously considers the general recommendations because they enhance the quality of performance institute wide.

Concerned faculty and staff members implement the specific recommendations mentioned in the external AA report. They also follow the same rule that is taking corrective actions at input, processes and output. They also observe the problem prevention rule. They prioritise the actions and implement them in order to bring maximum improvement in quality. For example the audit report mentions about use of innovative instructional methods for few subjects. The teachers should think about project method, problem based learning, action learning, industrial training and the like and prioritise the methods that best suits to learning objectives.

The recommendations of internal AA report are discussed in the seminar or workshop and it is a learning experience from good practices and deficiencies of the institutional members. Institutional members implement the learning from internal AA in next cycle of implementation. The internal AA report may reveal functional, resources and lack of competence problems. The management and institution should take it seriously to remove functional problems and gaps.

The informal AA process includes self-audit and peer audit it is a learning exercise for the institutional members. They immediately take corrective actions based on their learning and reflection. They develop and refine skills to deliver quality instructions, conduct quality researches and produce learning resources. These skills are used for further improving the quality of instructions. The internal informal audit creates quality culture in the functioning of the institution. It develops capability and capacity of institutional members to deliver more and better quality instructions. The improvement in quality of instruction in one course automatically brings improvement in other courses so internal informal audit creates a *chain and spiral* effect for quality improvement.

20. Which Guidelines should be followed by Institution for effectively conducting the Academic Audit ?

The formal AA is conducted systematically and in planned manner. The institution management should take initiative to plan and conduct the AA. A trained team of institutional members undertakes this exercise in a planned way. The AA team should observe guidelines stated in Exhibit 1.18.

Exhibit 1.18 : Guidelines for Conducting AA

1. Define the scope and terms of reference of AA.
2. Collect all necessary reference documents for conducting AA.
3. Conduct a meeting of all auditors and decide the approach of conducting the AA.
4. Prepare a comprehensive plan for conducting the AA.
5. Inform all the auditees of the institute through a meeting or circular about the audit schedule and preparation to be made.
6. Greet the auditees before starting the AA.
7. Conduct the AA according to schedule observing the code of conduct of auditors.
8. Note down the information and references for reporting purpose.
9. Provide significant summary points and validate them.
10. Thank the auditees for their cooperation and support.

Contd.

Exhibit 1.18 : *Contd.*

11. Conduct the audit of all the departments and sections allocated to you.
12. Prepare a compiled report of internal audit of the institution.
13. Discuss the report with management and finalize it.
14. Conduct a one day seminar on findings and recommendations of AA report for taking corrective, improvement and value addition initiates.

21. What could be the Nature of Resistance to Academic Audit ?

The resistance and its intensity to academic audit depend on institution and environment specific factors. The general nature of the resistance is stated below :

- Ignorance by institutional members;
- Non-acceptance by institutional resources;
- Lack of training in academic audit;
- Lack of resources to assure quality;
- Poor quality culture;
- Ad hoc quality system;
- Poor preparation for change; and
- No incentive and recognition.

The resistance is always positive and integral part of any change. It may bring out many new ideas which may be useful for academic audit design. The academic audit team should not avoid and suppress the resistance to change. It may help to identify the people who can help in design and implementation of academic audit. The academic audit team should use following approaches to deal with the change:

- Listen institutional members patiently about their apprehensions, doubts and issues;
- Encourage the institutional members to achieve goals, missions and goals of the institution;
- Increase their personal aspirations and ambitions;
- Provide adequate resources;
- Use shared leadership approach;
- Do small experimentation;

- Use participatory methods;
- Introduce rewards for excellent performance;
- Conduct awareness and education workshops; and
- Give specific responsibility to individuals.

22. Summary

Academic audit is a systematic approach to assure the quality of graduates of engineering institutions. The academic systems are conceived, designed, implemented and evaluated using scientific tools and techniques. The academic systems act as a sound foundation for assuring quality of learning of students at every stage. These systems help to make the learning joyful and reduce the time, efforts, and complexity in learning process. The academic audit conducted against the academic systems is useful in improving, enhancing and enriching the academic performance of the institution. It makes the institution responsive to satisfy the changing manpower requirements of the industry and society. Every institution should implement academic audit system for achieving the excellence. It may further be used for getting accreditation from NBA and other international agency. It may also act as an instrument for obtaining ISO certification.

23. Review Questions

1. Define academic audit.
2. Define academic audit systems.
3. What is not academic audit?
4. Define quality in relation to technical and higher education.
5. Define quality assurance.
6. Explain the model of journey for excellence in quality in technical and higher education.
7. State the purposes of academic audit at institutional level and individual level.
8. Define continuous improvement in the context of technical and higher education.
9. State benchmarking in relation to academic audit.
10. Define academic climate.
11. Define best practices.
12. Define value addition.

13. Define accountability.
14. Define empowerment.
15. Define academic image.
16. Explain the characteristics of academic audit.
17. List the benefits of academic audit at auditor level.
18. Define open system.
19. Differentiate between fast track and indepth audit.
20. Compare the benefits of summative and formative audit.
21. List the advantages of external and internal audit.
22. List the reasons for organizing experts audit.
23. State the benefits of internal audit.
24. List the parameters for fast track audit.
25. Compare academic audit with accreditation.
26. Compare academic audit with benchmarking.
27. State the assumptions for implementing academic audit.
28. Describe the academic audit cycle.
29. Explain the process of developing integrated quality and academic audit system.
30. State the norms for auditors.
31. Describe the code of conduct for auditors.
32. Describe the code of conduct for auditees.
33. Describe three tools and techniques for designing and conducting academic audit.
34. Describe the characteristics of the auditors.
35. List the competencies of the auditors.
36. List the documents maintained by auditees for academic audit.
37. Explain 360-degree academic audit.
38. Compare academic audit and ISO 9000 certification.
39. Describe the format of academic audit report.
40. Explain the impact of the academic audit on performance of the institution.
41. State the guidelines for conducting academic audit.
42. Compare performance appraisal system and academic audit.
43. List the training areas for the auditors.
44. Describe the model of introducing academic audit in higher and technical education.
45. Differentiate between academic audit and evaluation.
46. Compare the concept of quality control and quality assurance.

24. Activity for Auditors

Activity 1.1: Study the academic audit system of your institution in the light of the information given in this chapter and prepare a report on following points:

- Objectives of the academic audit.
- Process of academic audit.
- Training of auditors.
- Quality standards.
- Analysis of two audit reports.
- Type of audit conducted.
- Actions taken after conducting the audit.

2

Audit—The Vision of Your Institution

ADVANCE ORGANIZER

The vision acts as a guiding base for taking all major decisions for the institution. It is the source of energy for one and all working in the institution. It guides the faculty and staff members as well as admission seekers. It compels the institutional members to release their energy for achieving it. It is participatively crafted using creativity as well as logical techniques. It is widely shared by all related internal as well as external stakeholders. The right process of crafting the vision is very important because it seeks commitment, acceptance and empowerment of the internal as well as external stakeholders. So the process is audited for its quality and relevance. Similarly, the vision statement is very important for everyone related to the core business of the institution so it is audited on various characteristics. The criteria for process audit and vision statement audit are given in the format.

1. The Vision

The vision statement indicates the future intents of the institution say after 10 years what it wants to achieve in terms of customers satisfaction. It is expressed in future expectations of the customers and employees. It sets the aspirations and ambitions of the employees. It provides the clear picture of the destination of the institution. It is always stated in positive and enduring terms. It bridges the gap between present and future. Many institutions are expressing it in quality and value loaded terms. The vision is never constrained by current limitations, capabilities and capacities of the institution. The vision statement is described in words or phrases and not in long sentences and paragraphs. It is written in future completed actions meaning thereby as if it is achieved. Generally, the vision of the institution is constant but it forces the institutions to design dynamic strategies to achieve it. In some situations, the external or internal environment may change significantly and in that situation the vision may be irrelevant. In such situations the vision is refined or revised or modified or totally changed. It depends on the external and internal environment of the institution.

2. The Power of Vision

The shared vision for any institution has got tremendous potential to release the full energy of its employees to achieve it. Every moment, it motivates and encourages employees to use their full potential to achieve it. They have purpose and reasons to work for it. They attach themselves with the vision. They prepare strategic plan, perspective plan and annual plan to achieve the vision of the institution. It develops integrity, cooperation, coordination, collaborations, trust and networks among the institutional members. It creates opportunities for the institutional members to identify, develop and harness their potential for the core business of the institution and their self-satisfaction. It provides directions to take effective decisions where there is no scope for waste of time, efforts, money and resources on trivial activities. It increases the potential of employees to work in challenging and unfamiliar situations to grab the opportunities for the benefit of the institution. It guides the employees to set high aspirations and challenging goals. It prevents negative thinking, conflict, confusion and weak performance.

It becomes the base for influencing the stakeholders to collaborate, cooperate and network with the institution. It compels stakeholders to share their resources and expertise for achieving the vision. It attracts the customers to receive the products and services or both. The vision statement is considered to be the reference for taking any decision. The vision aligned policies, guidelines, norms, ethics, values, beliefs and culture is evolved to support the effective implementation of vision reach strategies. It guides the planning, organising, influencing, decision-making, controlling and rewarding functions of the organisation. The vision is a source and base for communication for one and all within and outside the institution.

Now-a-days the whole concept of having a vision for the development of the institution is diluted. The power of visioning is diluted by those who do not know the power of having the shared vision. Now people take it lightly and criticize that you have a vision or you don't, it does not matter much.

I have been an instrument in crafting the vision statement for some institutions. I remember the vision statement of all the institutions in which

I was involved. The two vision statements always impress me. They are "self-dependent village through balanced biodiversity". It was crafted involving all the stakeholders of a forest division. It says that the villagers and stakeholders will make the village self-dependent without harming the biodiversity of the forest. The forest division planned its all actions aligned to this vision statement. The other vision statement is of an engineering college it goes like "Hundred per cent placement in national and multinational companies". This engineering college reorganized its curriculum, curriculum implementation, assessment of learning, and faculty and staff members to satisfy the engineering graduate requirements of national and multinational companies.

3. The Trend

In past few years, many institutions crafted their vision. The institutions not having the vision statement are seen as primitive. So most of the institutions that are not having the vision statement used cut and paste technology to prepare the vision without understanding the meaning of the vision. To impress the visitors, customers and stakeholders they pasted the vision statement at all prominent places of the institution and printed it on all significant documents. The person or the group of persons who have prepared it using cut and paste technology and keeping flowery, attractive, catchy, and professional words in it do not know even the meaning of the words in relation to their institution. The vision statement appears everywhere in the institution without any impression in the minds of the employees on its relevance and significance for the institution. The contrary actions to vision statement can be seen in many institutions. Most of the institutions are suffering from fashion of vision. I call it fashion because they have it to exhibit to others that they also have vision statement. I had an opportunity of interacting with governing body members, directors, principals and faculty members of engineering colleges on vision statement, they say that they have a vision but when it is asked to reiterate it they say that it is written in Director's chamber and displayed at prominent places of the institution. They fail to reiterate it because they do not attach themselves to the vision statement. Having any flowery written vision statement cannot help any institution to excel better. It is merely a dream. Many vision statements appear like slogan, ethics, prophecy and philosophy. They do not indicate future state of the institution.

4. The Vision Crafting Approach

The vision statement for any institution is developed using variety of approaches, tools and techniques. In the process of crafting the vision statement, I consider that all the employees, stakeholders, customers and experts are invited to participate in creativity sessions on generating ideas for crafting the vision statement. This process of involvement of one and all makes people commit to their ideas and promises. The vision statement is crafted based on the hundreds of ideas generated during creativity sessions. The umbrella technique is used to classify and incorporate the ideas of employees and stakeholders in the vision statement. The broader and holistic words are used to incorporate these ideas in the vision statement. The umbrella technique is illustrated in Fig 2.1.

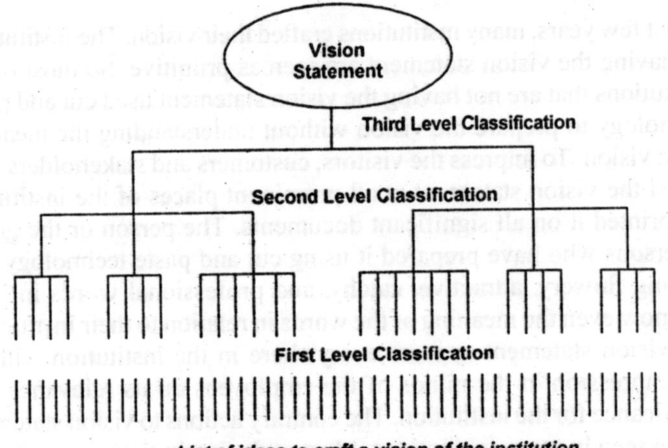

Fig. 2.1 : Umbrella Technique to Classify Creative Ideas

Once the vision statement is prepared based on creative ideas, it is discussed with the original participants of the creativity sessions and further refined. At the same time this vision statement is assessed against the strengths, weaknesses, opportunities, and threats of the institution and further refined. It is also assessed against significant issues and values of the institution. Based on these criteria and following the processes it is further refined for wider acceptance. Then it is communicated to the larger population of the stakeholders, experts, customers and employees for further refinement and acceptance. Again it is finally refined based on the comments of the wider population and approved by competent authority. The institution prepares strategic, perspective and annual plan to achieve the vision.

5. The Vision Audit

The audit of the vision can be conducted on two dimensions. One dimension is related to the process of crafting the vision statement and the other dimension is related to quality of vision statement. The process of crafting the vision statement is audited on the criteria stated in Format 2.1. The other dimension is related to the vision statement itself. The vision statement audit is conducted using the criteria stated in Format 2.2. The vision audit can be carried out by representatives of students, parents, employers, professional body, statutory body and other significant stakeholders. The vision audit can also be conducted by representatives of faculty and staff members from all the levels of the intuition. There are 10 criteria for auditing the process of crafting the vision. If the average of weightage given by auditors on process is more than 37.5, it can be considered that the process of visioning was worst. If the weightage is less than 12.5 it can be considered that the process used for crafting the vision statement was excellent. Similarly, if the average of weightage given by all the auditors on vision statement is more than 150, it can be considered that the vision statement is worst. If the weightage is less than 50 it can be considered that the vision statement is excellent.

6. Conclusion

The vision audit is a powerful tool to review the process of visioning and quality of the vision of the institution. The vision audit helps to analyse the weaknesses in the process of crafting the vision statement and quality of vision statement. The vision audit may help the institution to revise, refine, modify and even recraft the vision statement which is relevant to time and context and beneficial to the institution.

7. Formats

Audit the Process of Crafting the Vision Statement

Instructions for Auditors : Audit the process of crafting the vision statement. The process of crafting the vision is audited on criteria stated in the Format 2.1. During the audit of process of crafting the vision, if you come across deficiencies/gaps/weaknesses, note down the extent of gap in column 3 and description of the gap in column 4 of the Format 2.1. After examining the complete process of crafting the vision of the institution against each criterion and noting down the deficiencies/gaps/weaknesses think about the strategies to bring improvements in vision crafting process on various criteria and note it down in column 5. You can think about value additions with respect to the criteria under consideration even if you do not find any weakness, and mention it in column 5. Please use following scale for indicating extent of deficiencies/gaps/weaknesses in column 3.

- 5 – indicates very high deficiency/gap/weakness,
- 4 – indicates high deficiency/gap/weakness,
- 3 – indicates medium deficiency/gap/weakness,
- 2 – indicates low deficiency/gap/weakness,
- 1 – indicates very low deficiency/gap/weakness, and
- 0 – indicates no deficiency/gap/weakness.

Format 2.1 : Audit —The Process of Crafting the Vision Statement

Sl. No.	*Criteria*	*Extent of Gaps*	*Description of Gaps or scope for improvement*	*Strategies to bring improvement*
1	*2*	*3*	*4*	*5*
1.	Involvement of ➢ Faculty and staff members ➢ Students ➢ Employers ➢ Alumni ➢ Stakeholders ➢ Professional body ➢ Statutory body ➢ Experts in the process of crafting the vision			
2.	Effectiveness of conducting creativity sessions			
3.	Innovativeness in ideas for crafting the vision statement			

Format 2.1 : *Contd.*

Sl. No.	*Criteria*	*Extent of Gaps*	*Description of Gaps or scope for improvement*	*Strategies to bring improvement*
1	*2*	*3*	*4*	*5*
4	Professionalism in doing SWOT analysis, issue analysis and value analysis			
5	Diversity in analysing the issues			
6	Adequacy of values aligned to vision			
7	Consensus of stakeholders on vision statement			
8	Communication and understanding about vision statement			
9	Commitment and resolution of management and employees to vision achievement			
10	The concerns of people heard			

Audit the Quality of Vision Statement

Instructions for Auditors : Revisit the vision statement of your institution and audit it on the criteria stated in the Format 2.2. During the audit of vision statement, if you come across deficiencies/gaps/weaknesses, note down the extent of gap in column 3 and description of the gap in column 4 of the Format 2.2. After auditing the vision statement against each criteria and noting down the deficiencies/gaps/weaknesses think about the improvements in vision statement in the light of various criteria and note it down in column 5. You can think about value additions with respect to the criteria under consideration even if you do not find any weakness, and mention it in column 5. Please use the following scale for indicating extent of deficiencies/gaps/weaknesses in column 3.

- 5 – indicates very high deficiency/gap/weakness,
- 4 – indicates high deficiency/gap/weakness,
- 3 – indicates medium deficiency/gap/weakness,
- 2 – indicates low deficiency/gap/weakness,
- 1 – indicates very low deficiency/gap/weakness, and
- 0 – indicates no deficiency/gap/weakness.

Format 2.2 : Audit —The Quality of Vision Statement

Sl. No.	*Criteria*	*Extent of Gaps*	*Description of Gaps or scope for improvement*	*Strategies to bring improvement*
1	*2*	*3*	*4*	*5*
1.	Customer focused			
2.	Attractive			
3.	Broad			
4.	Compelling			
5.	Enduring			
6.	Shared			
7.	Inspiring			
8.	Memorable			
9.	Value loaded			
10.	Unite people			
11.	Comprehensive but precise			
12.	Magical			
13.	Unique			
14.	Well articulated			
15.	Plausible			
16.	Foster creativity and innovations			
17.	Challenging			
18.	Idealistic			
19.	Clearly understood			
20.	Key to leadership			

8. Review Questions

1. Define the vision.
2. State the period for which the vision statement is crafted.
3. Explain the difference between vision, mission and goal.
4. Describe the process of crafting the vision statement for a college or university.
5. State the tools and techniques used for crafting the vision statement.

6. List ten characteristics of vision statement.
7. Explain the powers of having vision statement.
8. State the five uses of vision statement for higher and technical institutions.
9. State the relationship between quality and vision.
10. List the stakeholders involved in visioning process.
11. State the criteria for selecting the experts for crafting vision statement.
12. List the approaches being followed by higher and technical institution for crafting the vision statement.
13. Explain the umbrella technique of arriving at vision statement.
14. State ten criteria for auditing the process of crafting the vision statement.
15. State ten criteria for auditing the vision statement.
16. Name two creativity techniques used for crafting the vision statement.

9. Activities for Auditors

Activity 2.1 : Craft a vision statement for one educational institution.
Activity 2.2 : Chart the process of crafting the vision statement of one educational institution.
Activity 2.3 : Audit the process of crafting a vision statement of one educational institution.
Activity 2.4 : Audit the vision statement of one educational institution.

3

Audit–The Organizational Structure

ADVANCE ORGANIZER

The organizational structure plays a significant role in facilitating effective and efficient functioning of technical institutions. It is designed to facilitate the professional performance at institution level and satisfy the expectations of students, employers, professional bodies, statutory bodies, and society at large. At the same time it should satisfy the faculty and staff members to perform effectively, efficiently, and professionally to achieve the objectives and goals of the institution. In long run the organizational structure should facilitate the accomplishment of missions and vision of the institution.

1. Rationale

The technical institutions are expected to perform variety of roles in order to satisfy the expectations of the students, employers, statutory body, and stakeholders. They are also expected to satisfy changing expectations of students and employers because of technological, financial and social changes taking place in the employer's organization. The scientifically designed and practiced organizational structure facilitates the effective and efficient functioning of the institution for satisfying the expectations of the stakeholders and delighting them. At the same time it facilitates the professional performance at individual and teams level.

2. Expectations of Stakeholders from the Institution

The technical institutions are functioning in a fluid environment because major technological, economical, social and political changes are taking place within the country and all over the globe. These changes are significantly influencing the expectations of the students, employers, professional bodies and stakeholders. The technical institutions are experiencing unprecedented pressure from stakeholders. The major expectations of significant stakeholders are stated below:

Students

The students are matured in learning process. They are well versed with the information technology, education technology and teaching learning methods. They are aware about world of work and have expectations according to the same. They take admission in the institution with specific vision, ambitions, aspirations, and needs. Different students have different vision, ambitions, aspirations and needs. They expect from technical institutions to professionally satisfy their expectations in joyful manner.

Employers

The employers of engineering graduates are undergoing tremendous changes because of changing environment pressure and throat cutting competition. They expect technical institutions to produce competent, proficient, effective, efficient and satisfying graduates. They expect that graduates possess competencies such as technical, entrepreneurial, managerial, research, social, linguistic, coping, risk taking, learning to learn, thinking, emotional intelligence, and the like. They also expect that graduates possess competencies such as accepting the challenges of the profession, working in teams, problem solving and decision making, negotiating, collaborating, cooperating, influencing, initiating, adjusting and forgetting fast.

Professional Body

The professional body expects the institutions to adhere to the standards and ethics of the professions. They expect that the institutions organize the activities promoted by them and contribute to the body of knowledge of the profession. They expect involvement of the institutions in undertaking collaborative activities for the development of the profession.

Statutory Body

Statutory body like All India Council for Technical Education, National Board of Accreditation expects institutions to function legally observing the laws of the country. They expect that institutions provide quality education and adhere to norms and standards declared by them. They expect institutions to do experimentation and evolve best practices for others to follow. They expect institutions to cooperate and contribute in activities, schemes, projects and programmes undertaken by them.

Society at Large

Society at large expects technical institutions to produce star graduates who can professionally serve the nation legally and ethically for improving the quality of the life of people. It expects institutions to provide quality education at comparatively cheaper rate.

3. Role of Organizational Structure

The organizational structure of technical institutions should enable the individuals and teams to perform effectively, efficiently, and professionally to satisfy the expectations of the students, employers and stakeholders. The organizational structure should facilitate the functioning of the institution in the following manner :

- Encourage use of scientifically designed and developed academic, administrative, managerial, and financial systems to facilitate the smooth functioning of all academic activities,
- Foster transparency in decision making and functioning of the institution,
- Promote creativity, experimentation, innovations, change, and development in order to satisfy the expectations of students and employers.
- Promote readiness for accepting the challenges and risk taking habit for the benefit of the institution,
- Prevent wastage of time, efforts, and money of institution and students,
- Foster collaboration, cooperation, networking, mutual sharing of resources, and creativity among the faculty members, staff members and students for efficient functioning of the institution.

- Create opportunities for mutual encouragement, appreciation, recognition, development, and sharing of experiences,
- Foster effective communication among the faculty members, staff members, management of the institution and students,
- Address the problems and grievances of faculty members. Staff members and students at right time in positive manner,
- Involve governing body members, director, head of departments, deans, faculty members and students in improving the functioning of the institution,
- Create opportunities for mutual interaction, training, guidance, mentoring, coaching, feedback and creativity,
- Promote effective and acceptable decisions making for improving the quality of education,
- Enhance responsibility, accountability, and commitment of faculty members, staff members and students for quality education,
- Increase self-confidence of individuals and teams to work in new and different situations,
- Inculcate conducive, healthy, and favourable culture for improving quality of performance,
- Facilitate the process of utilizing and mobilization of resources,
- Empower faculty members, staff members and students to perform to their best, and
- Create opportunities for career advancement, role enrichment, job rotation, promotion and incentives.

4. Characteristics of Organizational Structure

The organizational structure should satisfy characteristics such as decentralization, delegation, empowerment, flexibility, autonomy with accountability, simple to understand and follow, formal as well as informal, organic, open, inter-relationship between individuals and team, direct and shortest communication channels, and clarity of authority.

5. Conclusion

The technical institutions should shift from hierarchical structure of functioning to teams' structure of functioning in order to perform their roles effectively, efficiently, and proficiently to satisfy the changing expectations of students, employers, professional bodies, statutory bodies and other significant stakeholders. The technical institutions should evolve organizational structure that facilitates human resource development on mutual basis.

6. Format

Audit the Organizational Structure

Instructions for Auditors : The organizational structure is audited on the criteria stated in Format 3.1 given below. During the audit of the organizational structure if you come across deficiencies/gaps/ weaknesses, note down the extent of the gap in column 3 and description of the gaps in column 4 of the format. After examining the complete organizational structure against each criteria and noting down the deficiencies/gaps/weaknesses, think about the strategies to bring improvement in the organizational structure and note it down in column 5. You can think about value addition with respect to criteria under consideration even if you do not find any weaknesses, and mention it in column 5. Please use following scale for indicating the extent of deficiencies/gaps/weaknesses in column 3.

Legend

5 – Very high deficiency,
4 – High,
3 – Medium,
2 – Low,
1 – Very low, and
0 – No deficiency.

Format 3.1 : Audit—The Organizational Structure

Sl. No.	*Criteria*	*Extent of Gaps*	*Description of Gaps or scope for improvement*	*Strategies to bring improvement*
1	*2*	*3*	*4*	*5*
1.	Decentralized			
2.	Delegation			

Format 3.1 : *Contd.*

Sl. No.	*Criteria*	*Extent of Gaps*	*Description of Gaps or scope for improvement*	*Strategies to bring improvement*
1	*2*	*3*	*4*	*5*
3.	Empowerment of people			
4.	Flexible			
5.	Autonomy with accountability			
6.	Formal as well informal			
7.	Organic			
8.	Open			
9.	Inter-relationship between individuals and teams			
10.	Foster direct communication			
11.	Clarity of authority			

7. Review Questions

1. Define the organizational structure.
2. State the role of organizational structure.
3. Describe the expectations of students and significant stakeholders from the institution.
4. Explain the characteristics of organizational structure.
5. List the five types of organizational structure.
6. Describe the benefits of teams' structure.
7. Compare between teams' and flat structure.
8. State the limitations of hierarchical structure for educational institutions.
9. List the criteria for auditing the organizational structure

8. Activities for Auditors

Activity 3.1: Study the organizational structure of one educational institution and find out its limitations and strengths.
Activity 3.2: Design the organizational structure for one educational institution considering its present and future business.
Activity 3.3: Audit the organizational structure of one educational institution using criteria given in the Format 3.1.

4

Audit—The Institutional Plans

ADVANCE ORGANIZER

Educational institutions prepare variety of plans for achieving the objectives, goals, missions and vision of the institution. For the first time the plans are prepared using visioning exercise. The output of the visioning exercise is the vision statement of the institution. The vision statement is translated into missions, goals and objectives. The institution prepares the strategic, perspective and annual plan to achieve the objectives, goals and missions and in due course of time it achieves the vision. The plans are prepared using variety of tools such as SWOT analysis, Issue analysis, Value analysis, Pareto analysis, Force field analysis and Action plans. The techniques such as meetings, discussions, workshops and creativity sessions are used to generate innovative ideas for designing strategies to achieve the objectives and goals. The process of planning is important because it considers the capability and capacity of all the institutional members in activities. At the same time the authority roles, responsibilities and accountability is made clear to them. The commitment of internal as well as external stakeholders is obtained for implementing the plans. The plans are the source for mobilizing all types of resources of internal as well external stakeholders. The audit of process of planning and plans is conducted against well-defined criteria to assure quality of plans and their implementation. The format for conducting the audit is suggested.

1. Hierarchy of Vision, Missions, Goals and Objectives

The vision statement indicates the future intents of the institution say after 10–20 years what it wants to achieve in terms of customers and stakeholders satisfaction. The missions are derived on the basis of the vision statement. A logical process is used for arriving at missions of the institution. The number of missions depends on the vision of the institution. There could be 2 to 6 missions to achieve the vision of the institution. On the basis of the missions the goals for each mission are derived. There could be 2 to 10 goals for one mission. The goals may be common to more than one mission. Similarly on the basis of goals objectives are derived. There could be 2 to 10 objectives for one goal. The objectives may be common to more than one goal. As it is evident from the example, that for achieving the vision many objectives are formulated.

Once the process of deriving the missions, goals and objectives is complete, the validation process is carried out to check the completeness and relevance. This process starts from objectives to goals and goals to missions and missions to vision. So top down and bottom up process is used to finalize the missions, goals and objectives. This approach of deriving the missions from vision, goals from missions and objectives from goals is called future to present approach of planning. This process is shown in Fig 4.1.

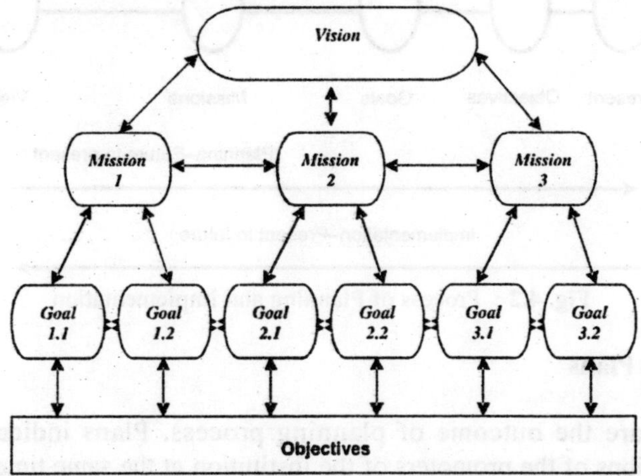

Fig. 4.1 : Deriving Missions, Goals and Objectives from Vision

The missions, goals, objectives are stated in the form of future completed actions. They are set to satisfy criteria such as challenging, innovative, specific, realistic, time bound, concrete, and worthwhile. All the missions, goals and objectives should enrich learning process of students and expand the academic business of the institution. They are expressed in quantitative as well as qualitative terms. The concept of benchmarking is introduced at this level to achieve excellence. The missions, goals and objectives are the source of designing strategies, taking major decisions, mobilizing resources, monitoring the progress and evaluating the achievements. These goals and objectives inspire one and all to release their energy for performing activities effectively and efficiently.

Once the plans are prepared they are implemented from present to future direction to achieve the objectives, goals, missions and vision. During the implementation of activities faculty and staff members put their efforts mobilizing the resources. The faculty and staff members cooperate, coordinate, communicate and work in teams to implement, monitor and evaluate the plans. It is important to note here that the process of planning starts from the future and the process of implementation starts from present. The process is shown in Fig. 4.2.

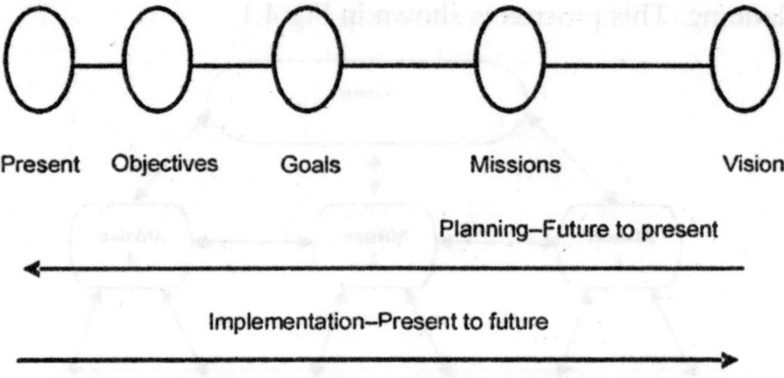

Fig. 4.2 : Process of Planning and Implementation

2. The Plans

Plans are the outcome of planning process. Plans indicate the aspirations of the promoters of the institution at the same time guide the actions of one and all in the institution. The vision, missions, goals and objectives guide the governors, directors and principal to take policy decisions about the future growth, development and quality of business of the institution. These statements are used to prepare strategic, perspective, annual and project plans of the institution. The institutional plans are used for departmental, team and individual planning. The relationship between vision, missions, goals, objectives, time and types of plans is illustrated in Fig. 4.3.

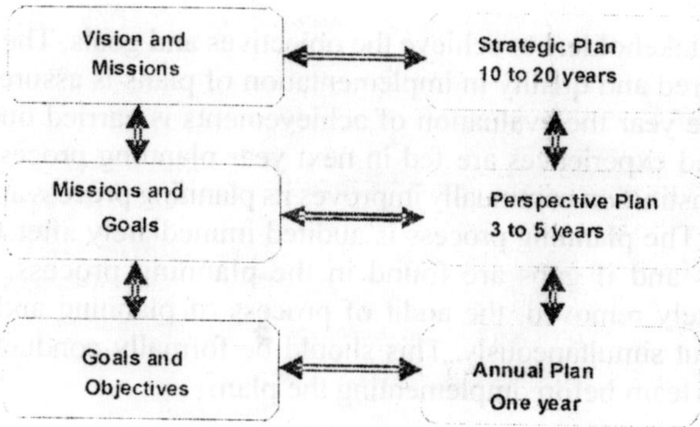

Fig. 4.3 : Types of Plans

3. Audit—The Plans

Plans are the outcome of the planning process within the institution. Planning gives considerable advantages over competitors to meet the challenges and work in uncertainty. The audit of planning process is important because it educates the governors, director, faculty and staff members about the challenges and opportunities for the growth and development of the institution. It is a process of educating the faculty and staff members on the core business of the institution. It helps to translate the expectations of stakeholders in terms of goals, roles and actions. It is a process of confidence building among the institutional members to accept the challenges, take risk and mobilize their efforts for achieving quantitative and qualitative objectives. It helps the institutional members to mobilize the resources and implement the change effectively. It helps to remove biases, prejudices, confusions and conflict related to functioning of the institution. It helps in minimizing the wastage of efforts, time and resources and thereby enhances the efficiency of processes.

Plans are the major inputs to performance of educational institutions. To assure the quality of overall performance of the institution, the plans need to be scientifically prepared, considering the present and future requirements of the students, employers, and society as a whole. Plans grab the opportunities available in the environment for the growth, development and excellence of the institution. They are prepared to remove the weaknesses and prevent the threats. Trained faculty and staff members of the institution implement plans in collaboration with external stakeholders to achieve the objectives and goals. The progress is monitored and quality in implementation of plans is assured. At the end of the year the evaluation of achievements is carried out and the results and experiences are fed in next year planning process. In this way the institution continually improves its planning process and quality of plans. The planning process is audited immediately after finalizing the plans and if gaps are found in the planning process, they are immediately removed, the audit of process of planning and plans is carried out simultaneously. This should be formally conducted every year by a team before implementing the plan.

4. Conclusion

Planning is one of the significant and first steps for professional governance and management of technical institution. It builds up the confidence of faculty and staff members to achieve excellence in effective and efficient manner. It is useful tool to communicate the intents of the institution to potential students, industry and other stakeholders. The concept of quality assurance, improvement and value addition in teaching learning process can only be implemented on the basis of plans. The audit is useful process for assuring and improving quality of institutional planning process and plans.

5. Format

Audit the Process of preparing the Plans

Instructions for Auditors : Audit the process of preparing the plans of your institution. The process of preparing the plans is audited on criteria stated in the given Format 4.1. During the audit of process of preparing plans, if you come across deficiencies/gaps/weaknesses, note down the extent of gap in column 3 and description of the gap in column 4 of the format. After examining the complete process of preparing plans of the institution against each criteria and noting down the deficiencies/ gaps/weaknesses think about the strategies to bring improvements in planning process on various criteria, and note it down in column 5. You can think about value additions with respect to the criteria under consideration even if you do not find any weakness, and mention it in column 5. Please use following scale for indicating extent of deficiencies/gaps/weaknesses in column 3.

- 5 – indicates very high deficiency/gap/weakness,
- 4 – indicates high deficiency/gap/weakness,
- 3 – indicates medium deficiency/gap/weakness,
- 2 – indicates low deficiency/gap/weakness,
- 1 – indicates very low deficiency/gap/weakness, and
- 0 – indicates no deficiency/gap/weakness.

Format 4.1: Audit—The Process of preparing the Plans of the Institution

Sl. No.	*Criteria*	*Extent of Gaps*	*Description of Gaps or scope for improvement*	*Strategies to bring improvement*
1.	2	3	4	5
1.	Involvement of faculty and staff members in the process of preparing plans. The techniques such as meetings, workshops, discussions, and creativity sessions organized.			
2.	Alignment of objectives, goals and missions with vision of the institution.			
3.	Priorities set among the objectives and goals.			
4.	Use of scientific tools and techniques such as SWOT analysis, Issue analysis, Value analysis, Force field analysis, Gantt chart, Pareto analysis, Alternative analysis, Stakeholders analysis etc.			
5.	Use of top down approach and bottom up approach of planning for preparing strategic, perspective, annual and project plans.			
6.	Use of proactive method of planning in contrast to reactive approach of planning.			
7.	Consideration of alternative strategies to achieve the objectives and goals.			
8.	Feedback, suggestions, problems and complaints are considered during planning.			

Format 4.1: *Contd.*

Sl. No.	*Criteria*	*Extent of Gaps*	*Description of Gaps or scope for improvement*	*Strategies to bring improvement*
1	2	3	4	5
9.	**Recommendations, and suggestions of evaluation of previous years performance is considered.**			
10.	**Timely preparation of strategic, perspective and annual plans emphasizing academic business of the institution.**			
11.	**Plans are communicated to all the stakeholders for commitment and implementation.**			
12.	**Resources are deployed for implementation of plans.**			
13.	**Strategies such as communication, negotiation, collaboration networking, developing core competence, value addition in the teaching learning process, and marketing are designed to mobilize the resources of stakeholders for implementing the plans.**			
14.	**The capacity and capability of faculty and staff considered.**			

Audit—The Quality of Plans

Instructions for Auditors : Audit the plans of your institution on the criteria stated in the Format 4.2. During the audit of plans, if you come across deficiencies/gaps/weaknesses, note down the extent of gap in column 3 and description of the gap in column 4. After auditing the plans against each criteria and noting down the deficiencies/gaps/weaknesses think about the improvements in plans in the light of various criteria and note it down in column 5. You can think about value additions with respect to the criteria under consideration even if you do not find any weakness, and mention it in column 5. Please use following scale for indicating extent of deficiencies/gaps/weaknesses in column 3.

- 5 – indicates very high deficiency/gap/weakness,
- 4 – indicates high deficiency/gap/weakness,
- 3 – indicates medium deficiency/gap/weakness,
- 2 – indicates low deficiency/gap/weakness,
- 1 – indicates very low deficiency/gap/weakness, and
- 0 – indicates no deficiency/gap/weakness.

Format 4.2 : Audit—The Quality of Plans

Sl. No.	*Criteria*	*Extent of Gaps*	*Description of Gaps or scope for improvement*	*Strategies to bring improvement*
1	2	3	4	5
1.	The missions, goals and objectives are challenging, specific, measurable, concrete, worthwhile, achievable, time bound, innovative, communicated, and understood by faculty and staff members, employees and translated into plans.			
2.	Plans focus on core academic areas and issues.			
3.	Plans are based on valid and reliable information.			
4.	Plans satisfy characteristics such as: effective, flexible, simple, cost effective, timely and plausible.			
5.	Focus on growth, development, continuous improvement and value addition in teaching learning process.			
6.	Potential problems are analysed and contingency plans are prepared.			
7.	Authority, roles, responsibility, accountability and duties are clearly mentioned.			
8.	Implementation, monitoring, resources deployment and evaluation schedules prepared.			

Format 4.2 : *Contd.*

Sl. No.	Criteria	Extent of Gaps	Description of Gaps or scope for improvement	Strategies to bring improvement
1	2	3	4	5
9.	Organizational structure created to implement the plans.			
10.	Problem solving mechanism established.			
11.	Assumptions are clear and manageable.			
12.	Healthy climate and culture developed to implement the plans.			

6. Review Questions

1. Define the hierarchy between vision, missions and goals.
2. Define strategic plan.
3. Define perspective plan.
4. Define annual plan.
5. Define project plan.
6. State the characteristics of mission and goal statements.
7. State the duration for which the missions and goals are stated.
8. State the number of mission statement written for an educational institutions.
9. State the factors on which number of mission statements depends.
10. Name the process for deriving the missions statements from vision statement and goals from mission statement.
11. State the concept of benchmarking in stating goals for an educational institution.
12. Explain the difference between process of planning and implementing.
13. State the fundamental difference between strategic and perspective plans.
14. List the criteria for auditing the strategic plans.
15. List the criteria for auditing the perspective plans.
16. List the criteria for auditing the annual plan.

7. Activities for Auditors

Activity 4.1: Prepare a strategic plan for an educational institution.
Activity 4.2: Prepare a perspective plan for an educational institution.
Activity 4.3: Prepare an annual plan for an educational institution.
Activity 4.4: Audit the strategic plan of an educational institution.
Activity 4.5: Audit the perspective plan of an educational institution.
Activity 4.6: Audit the annual plan of an educational institution.

5

Audit—The Curriculum

ADVANCE ORGANIZER

The curriculum audit for technical education institutions is a very strategy for taking the institution towards excellence. It is one of the methods to assure the quality of graduates being produced. It is a process to locate problems in curriculum, its implementation and evaluation. The chapter contains the evolving concepts of the curriculum audit. It serves variety of purposes. There are different ways of conducting curriculum audit depending on the basis of the objectives which is an eye opener for achieving highest level of quality. The guidelines for conducting the curriculum audit which is discussed here will give the desired results if followed in letter and spirit. The sample curriculum audit instrument provided in the format 5.1 is an attempt to help the readers to scientifically and practically carryout the curriculum audit of any engineering programme.

1. Introduction

The concepts of quality assurance, continuous improvement, continual improvement, value addition, re-engineering, and six sigma in the field of industry has enhanced the effectiveness and efficiency of the functioning of industry at the same time improved the quality of products and services thereby increased the satisfaction of the customers. In the quest of quality, a number of experiments are conducted by industry and audit is one of them. Learning from industrial experiences the concept of audit is being implemented in educational institutions. The curriculum management is the core academic business of any education institution. The quality of graduates is assured through scientifically designed, implemented and evaluated curriculum processes. The curriculum is the constitution of technical education system. Its proper implementation in letter and spirit decides its success or failure. To know about curriculum audit is one of the effective strategies to manage and improve curriculum.

2. Concept of Curriculum Audit

2.1 What Curriculum Audit is

The engineering curriculum audit is one of the methods to assure quality of graduates. It is a process to locate problems especially in curriculum implementation. It helps to define the problem and solve it. The curriculum audit is a systematic review of the aims, competencies, learning processes, learning methods, learning resources and assessment methods to compare the curriculum standards with quality of implementation. The curriculum audit is undertaken on well-defined criteria against set standards. A team of experts drawn from related disciplines undertakes the curriculum audit. Since the curriculum is designed with specific learning outcomes it is comparatively easier to conduct a curriculum audit objectively.

It is a systematic and scientific process of designing, implementing, monitoring and reviewing the curriculum processes, i.e. inputs, processes and outputs. It is a process of gathering information about implementation of curriculum processes of education programmes and comparing it to designed curriculum processes to draw conclusions about quality assurance of inputs, processes and outputs, i.e. products and services. It emphasises on reviewing the performance of the curriculum inputs, processes and outputs with an objective of quality assurance. It emphasizes on core academic inputs, processes and outputs as well as supporting academic inputs, processes and outputs.

2.2 What Curriculum Audit is not

The engineering curriculum audit is not a fault finding or assessment or evaluation process but it is a system for assuring quality of products and services of the institution. It builds quality culture around the core curricular processes of the institution. It helps institutions to align the quality efforts with the vision of the institution. It is not the review or assessment or academic monitoring or evaluation of the institution by statutory body against set national standards. It is a scientific process in which wide variety of tools and techniques are used by the institution to design the curriculum, implement the curriculum and ultimately satisfy the requirements of the employers and stakeholders in effective and efficient manner. It emphasises on participative design and implementation of curriculum in collaboration with industry and experts. The faculty and staff members are empowered to design, implement and improve the processes. In curriculum the institute concentrates on assuring quality, improving quality and innovating new dimensions of quality. The curriculum audit contributes for maintenance, sustenance, improvement, value addition and innovation in curricular processes to achieve excellence.

3. Purpose of Curriculum Audit

The curriculum audit is undertaken with multiple purposes:

(a) Improve, expand, innovate, redesign, add value, reengineer and increase the scope of the education programme.
(b) Compare the provisions of the curriculum and actual achievements and find out the gaps on well-defined criteria.
(c) Assess the level of quality attainment in different phases of curriculum life cycle.
(d) Identify the curriculum implementation difficulties.
(e) List the wastage of time, money, resources and efforts of students, teachers and institution in curriculum implementation processes.
(f) Obtain quality certification/accreditation from professional bodies.
(g) Publicise the academic image of the institution.
(h) Obtain various resources from funding agencies.
(i) Identify training needs of the implementers such as teachers, laboratory instructors, clerks, librarians, and curriculum development team.
(j) Design and implement curricular innovations.
(k) Assure the quality for next cycle of the programmes.
(l) Compare the effectiveness of the programmes within the institution and among the institutions.
(m) Market education programmes to students and industry.

4. Characteristics of Curriculum Audit

The curriculum audit should be designed to serve its intended purposes of quality assurance and improvement. The curriculum audit should have characteristics listed in Fig. 5.1.

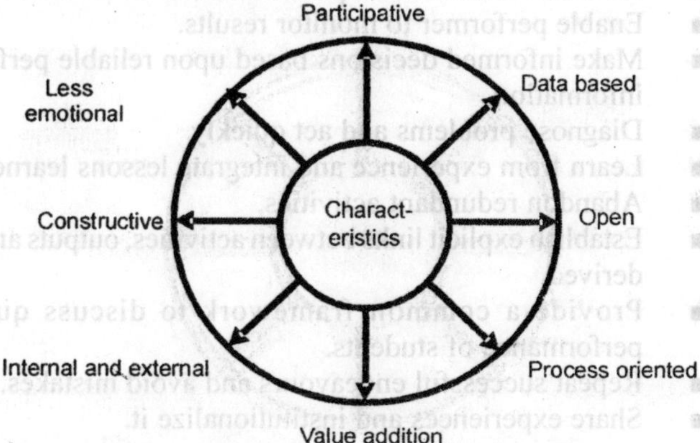

Fig. 5.1 : Characteristics of Academic Audit

4.1 Participative

Curriculum audit should be participative. All the interested persons should be involved in curriculum audit process. In the language of total quality management internal as well as external customers should be involved in curriculum audit. The institutional members should be involved from the beginning of the curriculum design process. Participation of institutional members in design of curriculum will enhance their commitment for implementing the curriculum.

4.2 Data Based

The curriculum audit should be conducted on the basis of factual data and performance standards set during the curriculum planning. The objectives are set for the semester or a year. In the process of objective setting all the significant stakeholders are involved. One can take data from various plans prepared in different areas of functioning of the institute. The performance objectives should fulfil characteristics, such as clear, comprehensive, specific to the performance, measurable (quantitatively and qualitatively), deliverable, in tune with the institution objectives, challenging, attainable, development oriented and observable. The curriculum audit should enable the individuals to produce benefits given as below:

- Have an element of empowerment.
- Enable performer to monitor results.
- Make informed decisions based upon reliable performance information.
- Diagnose problems and act quickly.
- Learn from experience and integrate lessons learned.
- Abandon redundant activities.
- Establish explicit links between activities, outputs and results derived.
- Provide a common framework to discuss quality of performance of students.
- Repeat successful endeavours and avoid mistakes.
- Share experiences and institutionalize it.

The curriculum audit is based on the principle, if we can measure performance, it can be manipulated. The quality of performance of teaching learning and other academic processes are recorded and records are produced during curriculum audit. It develops the habit of recording the data continuously in a systematic manner, which will provide continuous feedback regarding the progress of the work. This kind of documentation will be an evidence of progress.

4.3 Open System

The open system of curriculum audit not only prevents doubts and apprehensions about the quality but it also avoids the possibilities of bluffing, cheating and deceiving. People learn from good examples and mistakes of others. Open system helps to build up trust in interpersonal relationship. It provides an opportunity to exchange views on quality of performance.

4.4 Process Oriented

The curriculum audit should be carried out to measure the effectiveness and efficiency of the academic processes. It should focus core academic processes of the programme. Depending on the objectives of the audit the breadth and depth may be decided by audit team.

4.5 Value Addition

In every cycle it enhances the effectiveness and efficiency of processes. It makes the quality standards more stringent but at the same time achievable. In educational institutions the curriculum audit promotes joy, fun, interest, and humour. It adds value in academic processes as well as products.

4.6 Internal and External

Internal as well external members conduct curriculum audit with a purpose. Initially, the experts participatively design the academic systems and guide to implement it. Gradually internal members conduct the curriculum audit and bring improvement in the system. The members of the institution get variety of feedback from the auditors and learn to enhance the quality of processes. They receive feedback to improve their performance through training and development activities. Over the years, all institutional members get involved in curriculum audit activities of the institution. It is a very powerful method of installing quality system in the institution and obtaining quality certificate.

4.7 Constructive

The curriculum audit is introduced in the institution for enhancing the capability and capacity in delivering the goods and services. The introduction of curriculum audit is possible when it is constructive and focuses on improvement of the performance of the students. It is not considered fault-finding process but a process to promote mutual trust, appreciation and development for the quality of learning.

4.8 Less Emotional

The system of curriculum audit, based on facts and data, is helpful in providing constructive feedback to curriculum process designers and performers. It avoids the chances of incorporation of emotional parameters such as very old employee, performed very well during the crisis time, honest person, relatives of influential person, never oppose the decisions of management, traditional process and so on.

5. Types of Curriculum Audit Process

The curriculum audit is classified on various criteria in different ways as seen in Fig. 5.2.

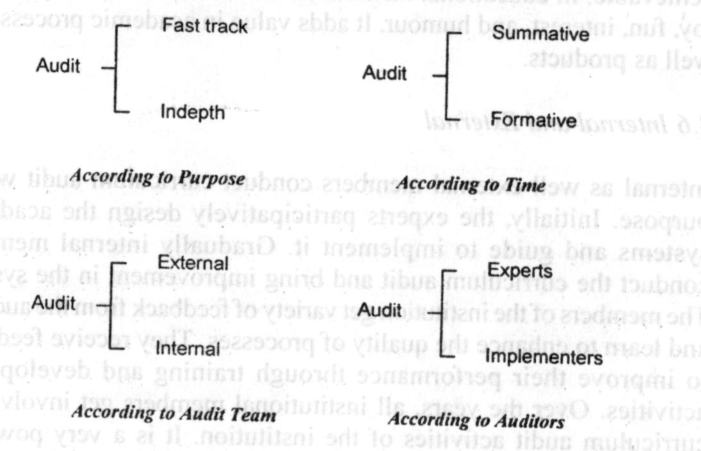

Fig. 5.2 : Types of Curriculum Audit

5.1 Fast Track and Indepth Audit

(a) *Fast Track Audit* : The fast track curriculum audit is conducted on significant curricular inputs, processes and outputs on significant and direct parameters to quickly know the status of the academic performance or any educational programmes. In fast track curriculum audit quantitative as well as qualitative parameters are considered for audit. It superficially reveals the quantitative as well as qualitative performance of the programme. The governing body or the management of the institution takes significant policy decisions on quality of implementation of the curriculum. It is generally conducted by experts and outside persons to prevent the biases in conducting audit and arriving at results. It is a sample and random audit of curriculum inputs, processes and outputs. The fast track curriculum audit is conducted for all the programmes of the institution on all the parameters of curriculum inputs, processes and outputs. The audit is conducted on randomly selected samples and on broad criteria. It provides the information for policy decisions and solve academic problems. The duration of audit is kept very short say one day. It is conducted after implementation of one cycle of the curriculum.

(b) *Indepth Curriculum Audit :* On the other hand indepth curriculum audit is conducted by the teaching and non-teaching staff preferably under the guidance of the experts. It is conducted on all the curriculum inputs, processes and outputs for improving the performance of academic systems on quality parameters and core curriculum processes. It is conducted by the person responsible for implementing the core processes and peers to provide and receive feedback on quality of performance. This is considered an educative exercise for one and all in the institution to assure quality, add value, improve performance, review process and take corrective and preventive actions.

5.2 Summative and Formative

(a) *Summative :* The summative curriculum audit is conducted by a team of internal as well as external experts drawn from various fields such as core discipline, education management, education technology, curriculum development, assessment and the like. The frequency of summative curriculum audit is decided based on numerous factors such as programmes offered by the institution, competition faced by institution, challenges ahead, demand for quality, time and money available for audit purposes and the like. The summative curriculum audit assures the quality of performance of curriculum processes for next cycle of implementation of the programme say four years. It is a holistic approach to assure and improve the quality of performance of the programme. Generally, the summative curriculum audit is conducted every fifth year. The institution takes significant decisions on quality systems of the institution on the basis of the results of the summative curriculum audit. The major decisions such as re-engineering the curriculum, recruitment of teachers, training of teachers, deployment and redeployment of the faculty and experts, infrastructure development, admission policy, development of instructional resources and the like are taken on the basis of summative curriculum audit.

(b) *Formative Curriculum Audit* : The formative curriculum audit is a continuous process conducted by institutional members for assuring the quality of performance of day-to-day processes such as effectiveness of instructional methods, practical, industrial training, project work, assignments, conferences, competitions, etc. It is a learning exercise for all the institutional members. The institution provides opportunity to its members for sharing the curriculum audit experiences in the form of meetings, workshops, seminars, feedback sessions and conferences. The members learn through sharing their experiences to improve quality of performance. In most of the cases it is an informal method of conducting the curriculum audit. The inputs, processes and outputs are refined, modified and adjusted on the basis of formative curriculum audit. It may be formally conducted every semester and informally conducted after every significant learning event, say after completion of every unit in a particular course.

5.3 External and Internal

(a) *External Curriculum Audit* : A team of experts conducts it to identify the strengths and weaknesses of the academic programmes and suggest improvement measures. At the same time it shares the best practices being implemented in various institutions with the faculty and staff members of the institution. It makes recommendations to modify the current academic system, design new system using information and educational technology and implement best practices. It influences the governing body and members of the institution to bring improvements in the academic systems.

(b) *Internal Curriculum Audit* : It is a process of auditing the performance of the curriculum processes by the internal members of the institution. It is a process of enhancing the accountability and commitment of the institutional members for implementing education programmes in totality and spirit. It develops the collective understanding of institutional members about the quality curriculum processes and their benefits. All the institutional members are trained to conduct the internal curriculum audit with reference to its objectives. It prevents confusion and conflict among the members. It also prevents deviation in conducting the audit and ensures effective communication. The internal curriculum audit is conducted observing the code of conduct/norms for conducting the audit. It is a formal audit conducted after completion of every semester. It is a sort of formative curriculum audit that emphasizes on observing the performance of academic processes. It points out the non-conformance to the systems and reasons thereof. It is a learning and improvement exercise for one and all in the institution. It also tests the effectiveness, relevance, efficiency, practicability and alignment of the curriculum processes with the institution goals and missions, if the systems are designed and implemented for the first time. The internal audit reveals the functional problems of the system at the same time specific methodology that works.

5.4 Experts and Internal Members

(a) *Audit conducted by Experts :* As described earlier experts are involved in designing the curriculum to assure quality, effectiveness and efficiency. The experts provide inputs from various dimensions of the quality to the design of the curriculum. They make aware and educate institutional members about importance of having academic systems. They guide the institution to implement the curriculum and enjoy quality. They are also involved in academic processes after one cycle of implementation of the educational programmes say after four years for undergraduate programmes and two years for post-graduate programmes. The curriculum audit conducted by experts reveals the system gaps. They provide latest inputs to academic systems design.

(b) *Audit conducted by Internal Members :* The internal members are involved in the complete process of curriculum implementation right from the beginning. They internalise the intent of the academic processes and their significance. It is the essential feature of curriculum audit because no external experts can assure the quality of implementation of the curriculum. The internal curriculum audit is purely diagnostic and formative. It is informal when implementers use it consciously to review the performance and take corrective or value addition initiatives on their own. It is also formally conducted with a purpose at the end of the semester. The internal members are involved in performing and observing the provisions of the curriculum as well as auditing the curriculum and performance. The internal curriculum audit brings variety of and numerous benefits to the institution. The significant benefits are refinement and perfection of competencies of all the members, continuous improvement in performance, corrective action at right time without intervention of management or external experts, sense of achievement and satisfaction, positive and constructive feedback, greater ownership for quality, building quality culture and enjoyment of fruits of quality.

6. Curriculum Audit Process

A systematic approach is adapted to perform the curriculum audit with the purpose to improve the performance of curricular processes and ultimately to produce competent graduates. The broad steps of curriculum audit are stated below :

A. *Constitute Curriculum Audit Team*
- Decide size of the team
- Set criteria for selecting team members
- Select team members
- Decide terms of reference
- Discuss with members

B. *Prepare for Curriculum Audit*
- Clarify purpose of audit
- Decide method of audit
- Clarify roles and responsibility
- Design curriculum audit instrument, e.g. Format–5.1.
- Validate curriculum audit instrument
- Decide format of audit report

C. *Conduct Curriculum Audit*
- Collect relevant documents
- Gather information from respondents
- Conduct interviews and discussions
- Observe processes
- Examine records

D. *Prepare Curriculum Audit Report*
- Compile information
- Interpret information
- Identify weaknesses, gaps, deficiencies, and opportunities for improvement
- Make suggestions for improvement

7. Guidelines for conducting Curriculum Audit

The curriculum audit is not an evaluation of the curriculum. It is different and undertaken with an aim to improve the quality of the programme to make it more professional and relevant to the industry and students. It is not a fault finding exercise. The curriculum audit team should be cautious about its behaviour while conducting the audit. The members of the team can follow the guidelines stated below:

(a) The curriculum audit is undertaken after completion of at least one curriculum cycle;

(b) Curriculum audit is conducted by a team of experts drawn from various fields, such as industry, curriculum development centre, research and teaching;

(c) The terms of reference for the audit are clearly spelt out.

(d) The audit is well-planned using scientific methods, tools and techniques;

(e) The audit plan is developed through mutual consensus between audit team and institution;

(f) The head of the institution informs the audit plan and preparation to be undertaken to the faculty and staff of the institution. She/he requests the institutional members to cooperate with the audit team;

(g) The audit team designs the method of audit, which is user friendly, takes minimum time, requires minimum preparation and efforts on the part of the institution, easy to conduct to serve the purpose;

(h) The authenticity of the information, which is collected, is validated with the head of the institution;

(i) To assure the validity and reliability of the information more than one mode should be used for collecting the information such as examining the documents, interviews with curriculum implementers, students, employers, parents and significant stakeholders, focus group discussions and observation of learning process; and

(j) The team members should not use jargons in the process of information collection. They should not ask for personal information not related to profession. They should not offer suggestions or comment during the process of audit.

8. Training Teachers for Curriculum Audit

Training of all teachers is essential for conducting the curriculum audit, for greater awareness about it. The programmes should be organised in the institution with the help of an expert team in which the following aspects should be included :

(a) Concept, need and importance of curriculum;
(b) Different components of a curriculum development;
(c) Approaches and methods of curriculum development;
(d) Design and use of learning resources for implementing curriculum;
(e) Design and use of learning methods;
(f) Management of learning in class room, laboratory, library, learning centre, work place and at home;
(g) Management of self-learning;
(h) Guidance and counselling;
(i) Maintenance of records;
(j) Networking and collaboration with stakeholders;
(k) Methods of assessment;
(l) Methods of offering feedback; and
(m) Quality assurance.

9. Summary

The curriculum audit is a systematic examination of curriculum planning, design, implementation and evaluation process. The main aim of curriculum audit is to improve, expand, innovate, increase, add value, re-engineer, re-design and increase scope of the education programmes. Curriculum audit is also undertaken to compare the performance, get accreditation, market the graduates, enhance corporate reputation of the institution, collaborate, network and seek cooperation of stakeholders. The institution prepares terms of reference for conducting audit and forms a team to conduct it. The audit is comprehensive and its scope goes beyond the academics. The process of conducting curriculum audit is a research work and a team of experts undertakes it. The administrative, managerial and financial aspects of the curriculum audit are addressed by other means. If these aspects are considered in this audit the academic aspects are overlooked. The audit team plans the method of conducting audit, conducts audit and prepares a report. The report is presented to the institution and the institution initiates changes suggested in the report for next curriculum cycle.

10. Format

Audit the Curriculum

Instructions for Auditors : The curriculum is audited on the criteria stated in Format 5.1. During the audit of the curriculum, if you come across deficiencies/gaps/weaknesses, note down the extent of the gap in column 3 and description of the gaps in column 4 of the format. After examining the complete curriculum against each criteria and noting down the deficiencies/gaps/weaknesses, think about the strategies to bring improvement in the curriculum and note it down in column 5. You can think about value additions with respect to criteria under consideration even if you do not find any weaknesses, and mention it in column 5. Please use following scale for indicating the extent of deficiencies/gaps/weaknesses in column 3.

- 5 – indicates very high deficiency/gap/weakness,
- 4 – indicates high deficiency/gap/weakness,
- 3 – indicates medium deficiency/gap/weakness,
- 2 – indicates low deficiency/gap/weakness,
- 1 – indicates very low deficiency/gap/weakness, and
- 0 – indicates no deficiency/gap/weakness.

Format 5.1 : Audit—The Curriculum

Sl. No.	*Criteria*	*Extent of Gaps*	*Description of Gaps or scope for improvement*	*Strategies to bring improvement*
1	2	3	4	5
A.	**Curriculum Planning**			
1.	Composition of curriculum design team			
2.	Method of revision of the curriculum			
3.	List of organizations that can employ the engineering technology graduates			
4.	Role listing, prioritization and classification			
5.	List of job/positions for engineering graduates in the industry			
6.	Professional standards in each role			
7.	Corporate culture analysis			
8.	Trends analysis in use of technology			
9.	Expectations and ambitions of students			
10.	Government policy			
11.	Expectations of professional bodies			
12.	Expectations of parents			
13.	Assessment of entry behaviour			
B.	**Curriculum Design**			
14.	Method of design of the curriculum			
15.	Aim and scope of engineering programmes			
16.	Assumptions for design of the curriculum			
17.	Method of recognition of prior learning			
18.	Roles performed in the industry			

Format 5.1 : *Contd.*

Sl. No.	*Criteria*	*Extent of Gaps*	*Description of Gaps or scope for improvement*	*Strategies to bring improvement*
1	2	3	4	5
19.	Procedure for admitting students			
20.	Classification of competencies			
21.	Learning Resources			
22.	Role of the student in learning process			
23.	Learning methods			
24.	Flexibility in learning with respect to entry, time, duration, exit			
25.	Competency maps			
26.	Credits for each competency			
27.	Curriculum document			
28.	Curriculum Implementation			
29.	Curriculum Theme Papers			
30.	Mechanism to solve curriculum implementation problems			
31.	Role of teachers for implementation, assessment and certification of competencies			
32.	Competence of teacher			
33.	Training of teachers for managing curriculum processes			
34.	Support facilities for curriculum implementation			
35.	Procedure of record management of students			
C.	Curriculum Implementation			
36.	Training of teachers to design, implement and evaluate curriculum on areas such as: • Curriculum design • Learning processes, events and experiences • Learning Resources • Methods			

Format 5.1 : *Contd.*

Sl. No.	*Criteria*	*Extent of Gaps*	*Description of Gaps or scope for improvement*	*Strategies to bring improvement*
1	2	3	4	5
	• Laboratory practices			
	• Learning at work place			
	• Assessment scheme			
	• Guidance and counselling scheme			
	• Offering feedback			
	• Curriculum audit			
	• Curriculum evaluation			
	• Work place training			
37.	Role clarity to teachers			
38.	Recognition of prior learning of students			
39.	Orientation of students for Curriculum and expectations of the institution			
40.	Design and implementation of instructional strategy plan			
41.	Design and implementation of lesson plan			
42.	Design of learning methods such as :			
	• Action learning			
	• Game			
	• Simulation			
	• Demonstration			
	• Problem solving			
	• Role play			
	• Creativity sessions			
	• Group discussions			
	• Panel discussions			
	• Focus group discussions			
	• Buzz group			

Format 5.1 : *Contd.*

Sl. No.	*Criteria*	*Extent of Gaps*	*Description of Gaps or scope for improvement*	*Strategies to bring improvement*
1	2	3	4	5
	• In basket			
	• Project			
	• Observation			
	• Assignments			
	• Seminars conferences			
	• Symposia			
	• Interviews			
43.	Use of above learning methods			
44.	Design and selection of relevant learning resources such as :			
	• Text books			
	• Reference books			
	• Installation and Service Manuals			
	• Handouts			
	• Assignments			
	• 3D-Models			
	• Magnetic cutouts			
	• Overhead Transparencies			
	• Power point presentations			
	• Self-learning packages			
	• Video programmes			
	• Multimedia packages			
	• Computer aided instructions			
45.	Use of above learning resources			
46.	Planning and use of laboratory methods			
	• Conventional learning			
	• Discovery learning			
	• Innovative learning			
	• Project based learning			
	• Assessment of learning			

Format 5.1 : *Contd.*

Sl. No.	*Criteria*	*Extent of Gaps*	*Description of Gaps or scope for improvement*	*Strategies to bring improvement*
47.	Industrial Training : • Overview of industry • Hands on practice • Problem solving • Innovations • Report writing • Assessment of learning			
48.	Use of self learning			
49.	Industry-based projects			
50.	Quality of communication			
51.	Students responsibility in learning			
52.	Action research			
53.	Use of learning resources utilisation centre			
54.	Assessment of : • Cognitive Skills • Practical Skills • Social Skills/Attitudes			
55.	Assessment of desirable/associative competencies such as: entrepreneurship, managerial, social, environmental, legal etc.			
56.	Time taken for developing the competencies			
57.	Networking, collaboration and support from stakeholders in implementation process			
58.	Maintaining record of learning			
59.	Certification of competencies			
D.	**Curriculum Evaluation**			
60.	Achievement of curriculum aims			
61.	Placement of students in industry			
62.	Job Position			

Format 5.1 : *Contd.*

Sl. No.	*Criteria*	*Extent of Gaps*	*Description of Gaps or scope for improvement*	*Strategies to bring improvement*
1	2	3	4	5
63.	Salary Package			
64.	Satisfaction of employers			
65.	Satisfaction of graduates			
66.	Satisfaction of parents			

11. Review Questions

1. Define curriculum.
2. Describe the concept of curriculum audit.
3. Explain what is not curriculum audit.
4. List the purpose of curriculum audit.
5. State six characteristics of curriculum audit.
6. Define open system.
7. Explain the concept of value addition.
8. State the types of curriculum audit.
9. Define fast track curriculum audit.
10. Define indepth curriculum audit.
11. Differentiate between summative and formative curriculum audit.
12. Compare the benefits of external and internal curriculum audit.
13. List the advantages of curriculum audit conducted by experts.
14. State the guidelines for conducting curriculum audit.
15. List the areas of training for teachers to make them enable to conduct curriculum audit.

12. Activities for Auditors

Activity 5.1: Develop the detailed curriculum for the subject you are teaching.

Activity 5.2: Audit the curriculum using criteria stated in format 5.1.

6

Audit—The Case Method

ADVANCE ORGANIZER

Case method is commonly and frequently used for developing higher-level cognitive competencies at post graduate and under graduate level educational programmes. Now-a-days each and every institution is developing its case bank through purchasing the ready made case study as well as developing the case studies. A wide variety of case studies are available which describe simple to complex and traditional to innovative situations. Teachers in higher education are specifically trained to develop and use case studies for assuring higher level of learning and integrating the learning of various subjects. Teachers are developing case studies on situations of interdisciplinary nature to integrate the learning of various disciplines to deal with real life situations. When case studies are combined with other methods of teaching learning affective domain and psychomotor skills are developed in students as a by-product of use of various methods without consuming extra time and efforts for learning. The self and peer audit of case method is conducted informally to assure the predetermined level of learning in all the students. The informal audit helps to refine the case study as well as process of use of case study. It is useful in improving the process of case method in next cycle of use. At institutional level summative and formal audit of case method is conducted to improve and innovate the quality of use of case method. A team of external experts and internal faculty members conducts summative audit. Formats for auditing the case study and use of case method are suggested for use.

1. The Case Study

It is a description of a real life situation about a problem or decision or crisis or task or conflict, or production failure or wastage or issue related to an individual or section or an organization or integration of all. This description is used for developing higher level of competencies of cognitive domain in students. The case is described on simple to complex situations depending on the learning objectives. In fact, case study is not an example, illustration, demonstration, game or incident. Case studies are available in written or recorded form. Case study can be developed by teachers to develop specific competencies. Case studies are developed using real life experiences, information available in documents, results of research studies. A case study may be written in the manner the role is performed in the organization and students are asked to perform the roles of the characters of the case study. It can also be written in interactive form in which the description of the situation is provided to students in phased manner. It brings the world of work in campus of the institution. The industrial and field projects completed by students of previous batches are the easily available sources of developing case studies.

2. The Case Method

The case method is a popular method of producing higher level of learning in cognitive domain. It is most commonly and frequently used method in management, law, medical, engineering and other disciplines for developing higher level competencies. The case method is versatile. It is used in combination with presentation, lecture, demonstration, group discussion, role-play etc. to develop a complete competency. It encompasses various instructional methods such as self reading and learning from the case study, role play on description of the situation, home or library assignment for finding the answers of the questions, assignment on development of a case study of real life situation, creativity and the like. It is used for inductive as well as deductive learning. It creates opportunities for active participation of students in learning process. It provides stimulus for thinking, visualizing and applying the previously learnt competencies. It develops the habit of exploring the information, collating it with the issue, analyzing the situation in broader perspective and designing the strategies. It helps the students to concretize the abstract concepts. It shifts the responsibility of learning from teacher to students. It is also used for guidance, counselling, assessment and development of students and employees.

3. Competencies Developed

The case method is used to develop wide spectrum of competencies that are essential for professional performance. It is used to develop cognitive competencies such as planning, problem solving, decision making, strategy design, evaluation of effectiveness of processes, investigation of a case, goal setting and prioritizing, assimilating, collating and comparing information to draw conclusion, trend analysis, forecasting, effective communication and presentation, guidance and counselling, reporting, assessment and evaluation, etc.

The case method is often used with other methods of instruction to develop associated skills along with core competencies. The associated skills are developed without any extra efforts, time and resources. For example, when it is combined with group discussion and presentation, the skills such as effective listening, mutual respect, receiving and offering feedback, appreciating the efforts of others, leading the group, handling situation, motivating others, resolving the conflicts, sharing values, trusting others, concern for others, responding to query, paraphrasing, obtaining commitment, developing a team etc. are automatically developed.

If the teachers develop the case study they also develop variety of skills during the process of development of case study. They develop skills such as information gathering with a purpose, classifying the information and presenting it, writing a story organizing the information, relating the theory with practice, investigating the situation in depth, framing issues for discussion, etc. They also develop the skills of transferring the responsibility of learning to students.

4. Audit—The Case Method

As mentioned the case study is a most commonly used method of instruction. It should be audited for assuring the quality of learning, its effectiveness and efficiency. In any management institution or engineering college 20 to 40 subjects are taught every year. If case method is used 2 to 5 times in each subject the figure comes to 40 to 200. This figure is quite high so the case method should be audited for improving the quality of teaching learning process and learning of students. The audit of the case method is conducted on quality of case study and use of case study. The case study is audited on criteria stated in Format 6.1. The use of case study is audited on criteria stated in

Format 6.2. The formal audit is recommended after every year by a team of external experts as well as internal faculty members. The institutions sensitive towards quality of education may go for internal informal audit of case method after every semester. Be it a formal or informal audit of case method experience sharing sessions related to use of case method should be organized every year in the institution for enriching the skills of the teachers for developing and using the case method.

5. Conclusion

The case study is frequently used for developing higher level of cognitive competencies. To assure the quality of learning of all the students, the case method should be formally as well informally audited. The informal audit of case method is carried out by self and peers against criteria suggested in Format 6.1 and 6.2. The internal audit is carried out informatively and learning from the audit is used to refine the case studies and method of use of case studies. The externally supported summative audit of case method is carried out at institutional level to improve and innovate the use of case method at institutional level in order to make the teaching learning process interesting, joyful and learning experience. The internal as well as external audit of case method is carried out on well-defined criteria as suggested in Format 6.1 and 6.2. On the basis of results and experiences of audit of case method training programmes are designed for the teachers to refine their skills of using the case method.

6. Format

Audit the Case Study

Instructions for Auditors: The case study is audited on the criteria stated in Format 6.1. During the audit of the case study, if you come across deficiencies/gaps/weaknesses, note down the extent of the gap in column 3 and description of the gaps in column 4 of the format. After examining the complete case study against each criteria and noting down the deficiencies/gaps/weaknesses, think about the strategies to bring improvement in the case study and note it down in column 5. You can think about value additions with respect to criteria under consideration even if you do not find any weaknesses, and mention it in column 5. Please use following scale for indicating the extent of deficiencies/gaps/weaknesses in column 3.

- 5 – indicates very high deficiency/gap/weakness,
- 4 – indicates high deficiency/gap/weakness,
- 3 – indicates medium deficiency/gap/weakness,
- 2 – indicates low deficiency/gap/weakness,
- 1 – indicates very low deficiency/gap/weakness, and
- 0 – indicates no deficiency/gap/weakness.

Format 6.1 : Audit—The Case Study

Sl. No.	*Criteria*	*Extent of Gaps*	*Description of Gaps or scope for improvement*	*Strategies to bring improvement*
1	2	3	4	5
1.	Suitability and relevance of case study for accompli-shing learning objectives			
2.	Match with the previously acquired competencies of students			
3.	Scope for use of previous learning in case situation			
4.	Attractive title and interes-ting beginning of the case study			
5.	**Description of case study**			
	• Related to contempo-rary real life situation			
	• Adequacy of information, facts and data to visualize the situation			
	• Based on primary information			
	• Effective linkages between events			
	• Flow of the case			
	• Easy and comprehen-dible language			
	• Interesting and involving narration of the situation which help readers to visualize and feel the situation			

Format 6.1 : *Contd.*

Sl. No.	*Criteria*	*Extent of Gaps*	*Description of Gaps or scope for improvement*	*Strategies to bring improvement*
1	2	3	4	5
	• Free from writers perception, opinion, prejudices and interpretations			
	• Free from grammatical and spelling mistakes			
	• Use of graphs, diagrams, tables of information,			
	• Effective conversation between characters			
6.	End of the case study			
7.	Brief			
	• Issue relevance			
	• Issue specificity			
	• Foster creativity and thinking			
	• Scope for discussion			
8.	Instructions for use of case study			
	• Time allocation			
	• Group formation			
	• Presentation of outcome			
	• Method of summarization of the learning			
9.	Notes to users			
	• When to use			
	• How to use			
	• Previous experiences of using the case study			
10.	Validated and Released			

Audit the Use of Case Study

Instructions for Auditors : Audit the use of case study on the criteria stated in the Format 6.2. During the audit, if you come across deficiencies/gaps/weaknesses, note down the extent of gap in column

3 and description of the gap in column 4 of the format. After auditing the use of case study against each criteria and noting down the deficiencies/gaps/weaknesses think about the improvements in use of case study in the light of various criteria and note it down in column 5. You can think about value additions with respect to the criteria under consideration even if you do not find any weakness, and mention it in column 5. Please use following scale for indicating extent of deficiencies/gaps/weaknesses in column 3.

- 5 – indicates very high deficiency/gap/weakness,
- 4 – indicates high deficiency/gap/weakness,
- 3 – indicates medium deficiency/gap/weakness,
- 2 – indicates low deficiency/gap/weakness,
- 1 – indicates very low deficiency/gap/weakness, and
- 0 – indicates no deficiency/gap/weakness.

Format 6.2 : Audit—The Use of Case Study

Sl. No.	*Criteria*	*Extent of Gaps*	*Description of Gaps or scope for improvement*	*Strategies to bring improvement*
1	2	3	4	5
A.	**Preparation to Use Case Study**			
1.	Selection/development of case study matching to learning objectives			
2.	Effectiveness of plan to introduce the case study			
3.	Generate alternative solutions to questions			
4.	Effectiveness in introducing underlying concepts, principles, strategies, methods, models, etc.			
B.	**Introduce Case Study**			
5.	Effectiveness in introducing the case situation relating it to theory, previous learning, and learning objectives			
6.	Effectiveness in giving instructions related to group formation, time distribution, sitting arrangement, expected outcomes, method of presentation etc.			

Format 6.2 : *Contd.*

Sl. No.	*Criteria*	*Extent of Gaps*	*Description of Gaps or scope for improvement*	*Strategies to bring improvement*
1	2	3	4	5
7.	Distribution of case and individual reading			
8.	Clarification of terms used in the case study			
9.	Providing additional information if sought by students and necessary			
C.	**Discussion on Case Study**			
10.	Effectiveness in conduction of group discussion			
11.	Notes taking of significant events during discussion			
12.	(i) Observing the behaviour of students on sociogram on various criteria such as content related learning of students, learning problems, depth of learning, linking of learning with other subjects etc. (ii) Behaviour during the discussion such as initiation, responding, listening, encouraging, strategy design, communicating, participating, appreciating the others, resolving conflict, summarizing, presenting the views confidently, convincing etc.			
13.	Encouragement and motivation of group members			
14.	Discipline and time management			
D.	**Presentation of Outcomes by Students**			
15.	Effectiveness of presentation by students on answer to questions, time, quality of presentation, discussion on presented answers			

Format 6.2 : *Contd.*

Sl. No.	*Criteria*	*Extent of Gaps*	*Description of Gaps or scope for improvement*	*Strategies to bring improvement*
1	2	3	4	5
16.	Managing controversial issues during presentation			
17.	**Summarization of Learning**			
	• Reinforcement of learning points and relating them to theory and practice			
	• Identifying the learning gaps giving additional inputs			
	• Flagging the issues for further exploration			
	• Providing specific feedback to individual students			

7. Review Questions

1. Define the case study.
2. State the classification of case studies.
3. List the competencies developed through case study.
4. Explain the limitations of case method.
5. Explain the process of developing a case study.
6. List the criteria for auditing the quality of case study.
7. Define case method.
8. State the steps of using case method for developing desired competencies.
9. List the criteria for auditing the case method.
10. What type of competencies are developed in teachers during the process of developing case study?
11. Which methods of instruction can be combined with case method?
12. List the by-product of learning using case methods.

8. Activities for Auditors

Activity 6.1: Develop a case study to develop desired competencies.
Activity 6.2: Use a case study to develop desired competencies.
Activity 6.3: Audit a case study using Format 6.1.
Activity 6.4: Audit a case method using Format 6.2.

7

Audit—The Industrial Training

ADVANCE ORGANIZER

The industrial training of students, teachers and instructors plays an important role in developing and refining the competencies. The industrial training should be organized professionally to take full advantages of it. In this chapter need and importance of industrial training, learning from industrial training and process of audit of industrial training is described precisely. The role of the teachers and industry resource person is described to effectively and efficiently organize the training. A format for auditing the industrial training is suggested. The outcomes of audit are used for improving the quality of industrial training of students, technicians and teachers.

1. Need and Importance of Industrial Training

Students having no exposure to learning in industry take longer time to understand their roles to perform professionally. They do not understand the work situation holistically and the importance of quality, effectiveness and efficiency. They do not willingly come forward to accept new responsibilities and challenges. They do not appreciate the complete role to be performed. They perform what is told to them and in due course it becomes their habit. They depend on other persons for trivial decisions and activities.

Management of learning in industry plays a significant role in refining the competencies of the students. They get an opportunity to come out from the campus and see the world of work. They see the application of theory in real life situation. They experience the importance of real life challenges, risk and problems. They get an opportunity to see the development trends in the industry. They see the complexities involved in the industrial processes. During industrial training students appreciate the need of positive approach, high value for quality of products and services, and performing professionally.

Another aspect of learning in industry is that the institutions and industries supplement and complement the business of each other. They are not separate entity. The industries share the responsibility to develop professionals and share the cost of learning through extending their resources for learning of students. The institutions have their own limitations of resources, hands on experiences and expertise. These limitations are also overcome through industrial training. The industrial training of students establishes a strong link between industry and institution to take up collaborative assignments for mutual benefit.

2. Learning from Industrial Training

The industry provides variety of learning opportunities for students. They get opportunities to develop and refine all types of competencies such as technical, professional, social, managerial etc.

They get an opportunity to see the use all types of technology and techniques to produce the products effectively and efficiently. The technical competence such as product design, selection of machine and tools, performing the job with accuracy, assuring the quality at every stage, taking measurements and recording them, improving the efficiency of performance and applying checks for quality etc.

They develop managerial competencies such as planning the work for achieving the targets, role allocation, communication, coordination, mobilization of resources, problem solving, risk taking, supervising, monitoring and evaluation, taking remedial actions, working without stress, working in uncertainties, rewarding and punishing the employees etc. in real life situations.

They develop social competencies such as establishing relationship with people at shop floor, leadership, followership, effective communication, asking questions, clarifying doubts, extending help, cooperation and support to fellow members, trusting people, sharing experiences, and so on.

They develop attitudes such as concern for quality, safety, saving, serving, house keeping, respect for others, cleanliness, record keeping, tolerance of undesired behaviour of others, positive approach to learning, and so on.

If students are placed for long duration training they learn to transfer the skills in new and different situations. They do projects, experimentation and research work. Students use all the senses in coordinated manner for completing the task and learning. The learning in industry incorporates various modes of learning such as learning by doing, learning by observation, learning through feedback, learning by mistakes, learning by experimentation, learning by thinking, learning by problem solving and so on. In fact, the initiation of competency development in students takes place in the campus and proficiency is developed during industrial training. The preference for a particular job is developed during the industrial training.

The industry resource persons use variety of methods of training such as demonstration, exhibition, role play, case study, hands on experience, problem based learning, discussions, presentations, assignments, projects etc. during the industrial training. The students are put under learning and thinking situation giving problems, assignments and projects such as to prepare a production plan, design a product, modify the product, refine the process for improving the efficiency, reduce waste, study and chart a complex process, design marketing strategy, reduce drudgery, design network, conduct failure analysis, diagnose problem, develop management information system, develop alternative solutions to achieve objectives, analyze risk involved, prepare presentation, design website, conduct audit of use of energy, conduct surveys, do comparison etc. These methods of training develop the hard competencies in the students at the same time soft competencies are developed because of use of these methods without investing time and efforts for soft skills.

The assessment of development of skills and competencies can be integrated with the industrial training. There is no need to take assessment tests because the progress on learning can be observed in natural setting on well-defined criteria. The learning is assessed on process of performance and quality of outputs prepared by students during the training.

3. Audit—The Industrial Training

The audit of industrial training is crucial to assure the quality of learning and development of threshold competencies so that students can take up the job right from the very first day. The industrial training is organized for students of all the students. The quality of learning is assured having well designed system for organizing industrial training. The poorly organized industrial training may result in waste of time, efforts and resources. It may not serve the purpose of learning. The industrial training is audited on the criteria stated in Format 7.1. The audit of industrial training is conducted every year by a team of teachers. The audit experiences are shared with all the teachers of the institution to improve the quality of industrial training of students. It is also used to improve the collaboration, networking and cooperation with industries.

4. Role of Teachers for Managing Industrial Training

The teachers should be trained to manage the industrial training of students. The trained and experienced teachers can better manage the training. They perform the roles stated below :

- Analyze the curriculum and identify the industrial training needs,
- Set learning objectives for industrial training,
- Identify the industry where students can learn effectively,
- Negotiate with industry and plan training,
- Orient the students on ways of learning, norms to be followed, learning parameters, expected learning outcomes, format of report, material to be collected, criteria for assessment of training, etc.,
- Assure quality of learning in industry through monitoring and review,
- Develop learning resources such as case studies, handouts, assignments, role plays, simulation, games, models, handouts on latest technology and practices, learning packages, and the like based on industrial training of students,
- Update the library, laboratory and workshop, and
- Undertake collaborative assignments.

5. Role of Industry Resource Persons for Managing Industrial Training

The resource persons from industry play significant roles in transferring learning and developing right competency in the students during industrial training. In fact they transfer their whole life learning to students in a limited time. They transfer the cream of the cream to students. They are the persons who create interest in students to enter in professional life with full energy, enthusiasm and creativity. They perform roles stated below :

- Appreciate and understand the learning needs and interest of students.
- Study the plan prepared for industrial training and design strategy to implement it.
- Organize orientation session and explain the industrial training plan to students and receive their comments, suggestions and expectation.
- Inform your expectations, rules regulations and norms to be followed by students during training and seek their commitment to it.
- Provide the written copy of the specific terms used in industry.
- Plan and organize learning events professionally.
- Assess the learning after each learning event and provide immediate knowledge of results that works as reward and source of taking corrective action.
- Demonstrate what of and how of competency. During the demonstration use actual machine site and exhibit your competency on it. Take the help of graphs, process diagrams and figures for demonstration.
- Explain all types of body movements and senses working to perform the task. After demonstration of set of skills provide an opportunity to ask questions. Then invite students to perform the task under your guidance. Provide opportunity for practice the skills to students. Assess learning of skills on the basis of process and product.
- Provide opportunity to master one set of skills and then move to next difficult set of skills and so on. Simultaneously integrate the previous learning with present learning.
- Create demanding and challenging learning situation having high expectations.
- Create learning opportunity to think creatively and apply knowledge, skills and attitudes to perform the task or solve the problem or to do small innovations.
- Always create suspense in learning process to increase interest and curiosity for learning.
- Promote intensive learning through stimulating assignment, problems and projects.
- Demonstrate, guide, support, help, and coach the students when it is necessary.

- Inculcate positive attitudes for confronting the problem, accepting the challenge, managing the crisis, planning and implementing innovations etc.
- Provide constructive feedback for improving the competency and behaviour.
- Share the experiences of professional life with students.
- Review the progress of learning every day and ensure that students are maintaining diary on learning.

6. Conclusion

The industrial training is organized to develop and refine threshold technical, managerial, social and professional competencies in students. The students get an opportunity to have a feel of real world of work. They integrate all the information, skills and attitudes to perform the task in real life situation. All the new models of curriculum emphasize on developing competencies using hands on experiences approach. The industrial training creates ample opportunities for enriching the learning process. The institutions are expected to network, collaborate and cooperate with industries on various issues including industrial training of students, technicians and teachers. The audit of industrial training will assure the quality of learning on threshold competencies of students so they become employable at right position at right time.

7. Format

Audit the Industrial Training

Instructions for Auditors : The process of industrial training is audited on the criteria stated in Format 7.1 given below. During the audit of the process of industrial training if you come across deficiencies/gaps/ weaknesses, note down the extent of the gap in column 3 and description of the gaps in column 4 of the format. After examining the complete process of industrial training against each criteria and noting down the deficiencies/gaps/weaknesses, think about the strategies to bring improvement in the industrial training and note it down in column 5. You can think about value additions with respect to criteria under consideration even if you do not find any weaknesses, and mention it in column 5. Please use following scale for indicating the extent of deficiencies/gaps/weaknesses in column 3.

- 5 – indicates very high deficiency/gap/weakness,
- 4 – indicates high deficiency/gap/weakness,
- 3 – indicates medium deficiency/gap/weakness,
- 2 – indicates low deficiency/gap/weakness,
- 1 – indicates very low deficiency/gap/weakness, and
- 0 – indicates no deficiency/gap/weakness.

Format 7.1 : Audit—The Industrial Training

Sl. No.	*Criteria*	*Extent of Gaps*	*Description of Gaps or scope for improvement*	*Strategies to bring improvement*
1	2	3	4	5
A.	**Planning of industrial training**			
1.	**Are the objectives of industrial training aligned with the curriculum and clear to teachers, students and resource persons from industry?**			
2.	**Are there well-designed industrial training guidelines available in the institution?**			
3.	**Is the industrial training well planned according to guidelines?**			
4.	**Are the guidelines and training plan communicated to students and industry?**			
5.	**Are the students given orienttation and instructions for stay, safety, discipline, learning methods, documents to be collected from industry, undertaking projects, report writing, and presentation?**			
6.	**Are the formalities such as consent of industry for training, agreement on schedule of training, role of different resource persons in industry during training, problem solving mechanism, monitoring the progress of learning etc. have been completed?**			

Format 7.1 : *Contd.*

Sl. No.	*Criteria*	*Extent of Gaps*	*Description of Gaps or scope for improvement*	*Strategies to bring improvement*
1	2	3	4	5
7.	Are the departments maintaining directory of industries related to their discipline?			
B.	**Imparting Industrial Training**			
8.	Overview of industry on its : Vision, core products and services, clients, brand image, organizational structure, size, turnover, profit, significant achievements etc.			
9.	Quick visit of the industry to familiarize the students with its departments, sections, people and technology.			
10.	Training as per schedule using different methods of learning such as exposure visit, demonstration, opportunity to practice the psychomotor and affective domain skills, assignments, project, problem solving, etc.			
11.	Quality of learning assignments, projects and problems assigned to students during training. Quality of output on assignments, problems and projects.			
12.	Opportunities given to students for asking questions, clarifying doubts, giving suggestions, notes taking etc.			
13.	Opportunities given to students for developing affective skills such as concern for safety, house keeping, concern for saving the energy, material and environment, mutual respect, concern for cleanliness, concern for quality, tolerance etc.			

Format 7.1 : *Contd.*

Sl. No.	*Criteria*	*Extent of Gaps*	*Description of Gaps or scope for improvement*	*Strategies to bring improvement*
1	2	3	4	5
14.	**Diagnosing learning problems through monitoring and removing learning gaps.**			
15.	**Quality of training, guidance, support and feedback provided to students in industry.**			
C.	**Evaluating Outcomes of Industrial Training**			
16.	**Assessment scheme clear to students and industries.**			
17.	**Quality of report prepared by students on industrial training** **General quality:** Complete, precise, logic, way of presentation, use of graphs, tables and figures, case study etc. **Technical quality:** Variety of learning events, problems and challenges of the industry and their solutions, opportunities for growth and development, technology and processes, specific project details etc.			
18.	**Quality of oral presentation on confidence, flow, linkages, language, use of media, handling questions of audience etc.**			
19.	**Quality of learning of core competencies.**			
20.	**Quality of learning on associated competencies.**			
21.	**Documents such as policies, manuals, work instructions, technical specification, process description, organizational structure, various formats, books, and material collected from industry.**			
22.	**Behaviour of the students during training.**			

Format 7.1 : *Contd.*

Sl. No.	*Criteria*	*Extent of Gaps*	*Description of Gaps or scope for improvement*	*Strategies to bring improvement*
1	2	3	4	5
23.	Quality of feedback given to students for refining the competencies.			
24.	Remedial treatment given to students by teachers for removing learning gaps.			
25.	Learning resources such as case studies, handouts, assignments, role-plays, simulation, games, models developed based on industrial training of students.			
26.	Consultancy projects such as continuing education programmes, problem solving, learning resources development, research projects obtained by institution.			
27.	Collaborative work such as organizing seminars, conferences, training programmes, research started by institution.			

8. Review Questions

1. State the need and importance of industrial training for students of higher and technical education.
2. List the competencies developed through industrial training.
3. Describe the method of organizing industrial training of students.
4. State the role of teachers in organizing industrial training.
5. State the role of industry resource person in organizing industrial training.
6. Explain the guidelines to be followed for organizing industrial training.
7. List the criteria for auditing the industrial training.

8. What are the limitations of industrial training?
9. How the experiences of industrial training of students should be used by teachers?
10. What should be the format of report of industrial training?

9. Activities for Auditors

Activity 7.1 : Prepare a guideline document at institutional level to organize industrial training of students, faculty members and staff members.

Activity 7.2 : Audit the industrial training of students using Format 7.1.

8

Audit—The Learning Resources

ADVANCE ORGANIZER

The learning resources (LRs) are one of the significant elements of teaching learning process. Their share is 50 per cent with respect to time in teaching learning process. The LRs are systematically and scientifically designed to enrich the teaching learning process, save time and efforts of teachers and students in learning process, change stimulus, involve students in learning process, and gradually shift the responsibility of learning to students. The LRs should be designed, developed and distributed by learning resources development centre (LRDC) constituted at national or State level to prevent duplication of time and efforts at national level. There are various types of LRs such as learning method, media, assignments and assessment. There are soft and hard and student centered and teacher centered LRs. Each type of LRs is used considering the requirement of the curriculum, learning style, availability of time and other resources. The LRs developed by LRDC are distributed to institutions spread nationwide. These LRs are housed in learning resources utilization centre (LRUC) in institutions and used by trained teachers and students to achieve curriculum objectives. Considering the importance of LRs these should be audited for assuring, maintaining and improving their quality at LRDC and institutional level. The LRs are audited on process of development, quality of LRs and their use by teachers and students using objective criteria.

1. Introduction

The learning resources (LRs) play an important role in enriching learning processes to develop intended competencies in all the students. The LRs complement and supplement the learning process. Traditionally the LRs are used to change the stimulus and break the monotony in learning process. LRs enhance the effectiveness and efficiency of learning process. Well designed LRs and their effective use bring variety in the learning process and create challenges for the learners. They are the strong tools to involve students in learning process and gradually transfer the responsibility of learning to them. LRs provide an opportunity to use all the 5 senses of learning and thereby accelerate the learning process.

2. Benefits of Learning Resources

There are numerous benefits of using LRs in teaching learning process. Some of the significant benefits are listed below :

- Teachers review the literature, reflect on their experiences and do research work so they learn considerably during the process of design and development of LRs. The learning of teachers gets reflected in teaching learning process. They become more confident and proficient in conducting the teaching learning process.
- LRs save a great amount of time of teachers because once LRs are developed they reduce the time of preparation and can be used repetitively.
- They substitute the teachers in many situations thereby the teachers get more time to undertake productive and innovative work related to teaching learning. To a great extent LRs can overcome the shortage of faculty and incompetence of faculty, which is prevailing in emerging disciplines.
- LRs save time of students in many ways such as time in searching for learning material, reading unnecessary learning material, listening to long lectures, participating in undesired learning activities, etc. Students become confident about their learning because they have relevant, effective, efficient and attractive LRs.
- LRs bring variety in presentations, learning activities, learning styles, learning methods, and assessment procedure thereby enriching learning process. LRs address the varied learning needs of all the students. They provide adequate flexibility for slow learners, fast learners, low entry behaviour and high entry behaviour students.
- LRs create opportunities to promote creativity, reasoning and thinking for all types of students.

- LRs based on world of work and professional life create importance and urgency for learning particular competency. LRs describing real life involve students in learning process naturally.
- LRs invite attention and interest of the students. The students have free access to the LRs, therefore, they can directly use LRs whenever they have need and mood to learn.
- The learning assignments such as reading, problem solving, role-playing, simulation, and discussions are based on LRs thereby involve the students in learning process.
- LRs encourage self-learning, collaborative learning, and mutual learning and foster synergetic effect in learning process thereby increase learning maturity of students.
- LRs are developed and used according to requirements of learning objectives and thereby assure quality in learning process.
- LRs are concrete elements in learning process, therefore, can be benchmarked with the best in the world. They are the base for value addition and continuous improvement.
- LRs both hard and soft can be carried anywhere by the students and they can use it any time. Students can use them in the desired manner. LRs fulfil the learning needs of the students and match with the learning styles. LRs can be used individually and in a group.

3. Classification of Learning Resources

LRs can be classified in variety of ways using criteria stated in Fig. 8.1.

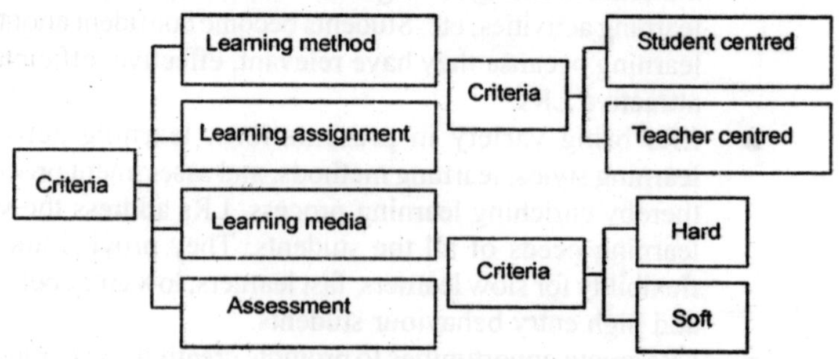

Fig. 8.1 : Classification of Learning Resources

According to Learning Methods

The learning situation is described in writing and distributed to the students. The description of learning situation works as a learning resource in the form of a handout. The description of learning situation for conducting learning methods such as Action learning, Game, Simulation, Competition, Demonstration, Problem based situation, Role play, Practice, Creativity session, Group discussion, Panel discussion, Focus discussion, Buzz group, In basket, Project, Puzzle, Assignments, Seminars, Conference, Symposium, Interactions, Interview, Question answer, Observation, Quiz are distributed to the students so that they can comprehend the situation and participate in the learning process. The description of situation brings real life in the classroom and laboratory. The learning method is designed on the points such as competency statement, skills to be developed, choice of learning method, guidelines for teachers to use, previous learning, handout (if any), time schedule, teacher activity, students activities, physical resources requirement, learning outcomes, criteria for assessment of learning, points for feedback and references for further learning.

According to Learning Assignments

The learning assignments are described according to requirements of learning objectives. The subject experts considering the requirements of learning objectives, entry behaviour of students and progress of learning design these learning assignments. These learning assignments are great source of learning for students because they create learning challenges for the students. Learning assignments create opportunities for thinking, practicing, reading, questioning, risk taking, planning, organizing, negotiating, problem solving, discovering, comparison, visualizing, testing, evaluation, winning, committing mistakes, using technology, appreciating, cooperating, collaborating, adopting, adjusting, modifying, refining, value addition, accepting, rejecting, opposing, reasoning, convincing, connecting, collating, linking, pursuing, influencing, respecting, stimulating, summarizing, instructing, concluding etc. Students refer variety of sources such as textbooks, reference books, manuals, codes, journals, reports etc. to complete the assignments. At the same time students get an opportunity to struggle for learning during the learning process.

- *Reading Assignment :* Self-learning resources, text book, handouts, research paper, reference book, e-book, computer aided instructions, multimedia packages, manuals, codes, guidelines, procedures etc.
- *Review Assignment :* Review of a book, research paper, design of product/process/structure/software, film, etc.
- *Problem Solving Assignment :* Solving theoretical problems, analyzing failure, industrial projects, trouble shooting, wastage reduction, inventory management, inefficiency, delay, wear and tear, etc.
- *Developmental Assignment :* Conducting survey, preparing a plan, designing a new product, designing software, writing a research paper, seminars, and value addition to an existing product, modifying the process to improve efficiency or effectiveness or both.
- *Report Writing :* Preparing observation report, investigation report, survey report, feasibility report, comparative report, accident report, impact report, study report, assessment report, audit report etc.
- *Investigation, Evaluation and Research :* Predicting the future technology, Application of theory in practice, research study for various purposes, evaluating the effectiveness and efficiency of a process, investigating a case, comparative study, analysis of failure, impact of a product or services. These assignments are based on some real life situation which are described and distributed to the students. This description of situation acts as a learning resources for the students as well as teachers.
- *Laboratory Assignments :* Various types of laboratory assignments such as conventional type of practical, discovery learning, investigative learning, problems, projects and innovations are designed and used by teachers considering the requirements of learning objectives in general and manual skills in particular. These assignments are well designed and described in written form to produce learning.
- *Field Assignments :* Field and industrial situations are described and assigned to students for producing learning related to learning objectives. This description of situation acts as a learning resource for the students.

The learning assignment is designed on the points such as competency statement, skills to be developed, name of the learning assignment, purpose of learning assignment, guidelines for teachers to use, previous learning, design of learning assignment, time schedule, teacher activities, students activities, physical resources requirement, learning outcome, criteria for assessment of learning outcome, points for feedback, and references for further learning.

According to Learning Media

Teachers use variety of media for transferring learning at various stages of learning process. These media are used to save time, create interest, provide flexibility and enrich learning process. Media are used to link the current learning with previous learning, provide advance organizer, define new terminology, explain the process in simple way etc. The media is designed using principles such as known to unknown, simple to complex learning, whole to part and part to whole, concrete to abstract learning, and present to future practices. It creates scope for analogy, contrast, question answer, assessment, visualization, and humour. It brings real life dynamic world in the classroom.

The media such as Textbook, Reference Book, E-book, Workbook, Self-learning package, Research articles, Power point presentations, Audio programmes, Video programmes, Computer aided instructions, Laboratory manuals, Handbooks, Observation sheet, Interview sheet, Check lists, Photographic album, Flip chart, Charts, Cutouts, Diagrams, Graphs, Models, Exhibits etc. are used by teachers and students during the learning process.

The teachers learn about theory and practice when they prepare media and students learn when they use media. The learning media is designed on the points such as competency statement, skills to be developed, name of the learning media, purpose of learning media, guidelines for teachers to use, design of learning media, teacher activities, physical resources requirement, learning outcome, criteria for assessment of learning outcome, points for feedback, and references for further learning.

According to Assessment

The assessment tools and techniques are used for assessing the progress of learning, diagnosing the learning problems, rewarding the current learning and adding value to further learning. In true sense the assessment tools and techniques are used as means of learning. The assessment is used as means of learning in following two ways :

(i) *Formative Assessment :* Class test, output of all types of assignment's output of learning methods, output of all types of reports, output of practice in laboratory, workshop and industry/work place, presentations, performance etc. are means of learning for the students as well as teachers.

(ii) *Summative Assessment :* Final test of competency—demonstration of competency and certification of competencies of previous batches and current batches are means of learning because they reinforce learning, diagnose learning problems and correct learning mistakes. The assessment is designed on the points such as competency statement, skills to be developed, name of the assessment method, purpose of assessment method, guidelines for teachers to use, design of assessment method, teacher activities, student activities, physical resources requirement, points for feedback and references for further learning.

4. Learning Resources Development Centres (LRDC)

There is a wide range of LRs that can be selected by teachers for achieving learning objectives. These LRs are designed by a team of experts to produce desired level of learning in students. The LRs are easy and interesting to learn, handy to carry, easy to use, attractive to watch, create enjoyment in learning, precise, concise, self-explanatory, complete, and aligned to achievement of competency. The LRs create interest, curiosity and challenges in learning process. They create opportunities for students to apply previous learning, explore the unknown, experience the truth and feel the joy of learning. They reduce the dependence on teachers and empower the students for learning.

LRs design is a much bigger project than curriculum development. The process of design of different types of LRs is different. The formats of LRs vary significantly depending on its purpose. If the curriculum is designed and implemented nationwide or statewide, the design, production and dissemination work is undertaken by a learning resources development centre (LRDC). The matter for LRs is drawn from the industry, research organizations, resource institutions, and engineering institutions.

Composition of LRDC

The greatest limitation with teachers working in different institutions is that they get less time to prepare the LRs because they are intensively involved in curriculum implementation and other related processes. They are not trained to design LRs that are technically, psychologically, and economically feasible for competency development. If LRs are designed in every institution, there would be duplication of investment, time, and efforts. There are chances of wide diversity in approaching the competency. It would result in national waste in terms of time, efforts and money. So it is suggested to develop the LRs by a team of experts for LRDC. A team of experts designs the LRs professionally and economically. It maintains uniformity, integrity, continuity, linkages and variety in LRs. It designs the LRs based on their experience, expertise and creativity. This approach of LRs development reduces the workload and time for developing the LRs in individual institutions. The LRs developed by LRDC are distributed to institutions spread all over the country. The institutions are encouraged to invest on using the LRs effectively and efficiently. However, they are free to design LRs on their researches and unique experiences. The institutions are provided an opportunity to share LRs developed by them with all the institutions through LRDC. The design and development of LRs require time, patience, creativity and efforts.

The LRDC networks with industry, research institution, experts, resource persons, engineering institutions, teachers and other stakeholders. It creates a pool of experts from all over the country. It prepares a panel of experts for each discipline, each subject and area of specialization. The LRDC should work with curriculum development centre (CDC). It should network, collaborate, and coordinate with the industry, renowned research institutions, centre of excellence, and media agencies at national and international level for obtaining world-class latest learning material. The experts are registered with the panel for developing LRs. It should have accessibility to all leading companies for documenting their practices and culture. The team comprises of experts from industry, engineering education, training, media and assessment. This team is supported by various persons to do ground work and support various academic, technical, financial and administrative activities. This team designs the LRs for implementing learning strategy to develop the specific competency effectively, efficiently and joyfully. The composition of LRDC at national level is shown in Fig. 8.2.

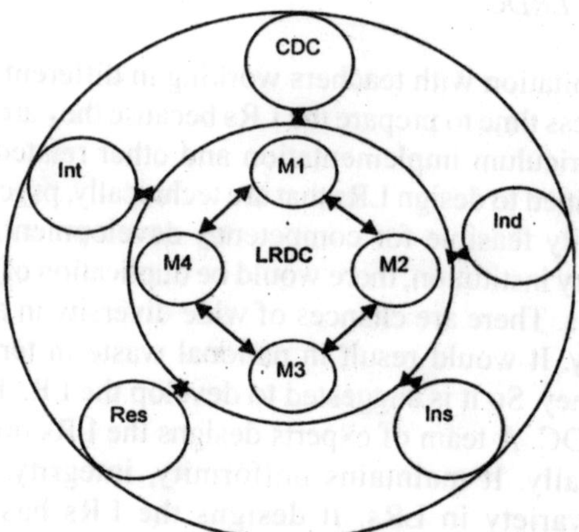

Legend : M1–Subject expert, M2–Industry expert, M3–Education technology expert, M4–Research expert, CDC–Curriculum development cell, Ind–Industry, Ins–Institutions, Res–Research, Int–International universities and resource organizations

Fig. 8.2: Composition of LRDC at National Level

Functions of LRDC

The LRDC should perform the functions as stated below :

- Plan and develop all types of LRs to fulfil the requirements of implementing the curriculum.
- Publish standard glossary for curriculum including technical terms.
- Impart training to resource persons to develop, refine, and re-engineer the LRs.
- Impart training to teachers and other resource persons to use the LRs effectively and efficiently.
- Suggest a list of hardware and software required to use the LRs in institutions.
- Organize seminars, conferences, workshops, and competitions on innovations in development of LRs.
- Market the LRs to the students, teachers, institutions and industry.
- Collaborate with research institutions, resource institutions,

industry and teachers for various purposes related to LRs development.

- Disseminate the LRs to institutions at right time.
- Motivate, encourage and empower teachers to develop and use LRs.
- Create LRs Bank for various types of LRs in each discipline, subject and area.
- Offer consultancy to industry for developing and using LRs for conducting continuing education programmes.
- Act as a LRs clearing house.
- Conduct research studies in the area of LRs development, implementation, evaluation and impact assessment.

5. Design of Learning Resources

The LRDC develops LRs using a project approach in which numbers of parallel activities are performed for developing various types of LRs in time. The LRDC plans this project to design and develop the LRs. Several trained teams in different disciplines and subjects need to perform the simultaneous activities to reduce the project duration. It is estimated that for each discipline 20 to 30 teams are required to develop the LRs. The LRDC designs and follows a standard process for designing, developing and distributing LRs of different types to different institutions. LRs are chosen from the curriculum document where it is identified and classified. They are indicated in the strategic plan, instructional strategy plan and lesson plans. If the LRs are not mentioned in the curriculum document the respective team identifies the LRs and develops them. The broad steps of design of LRs are stated in Fig. 8.3.

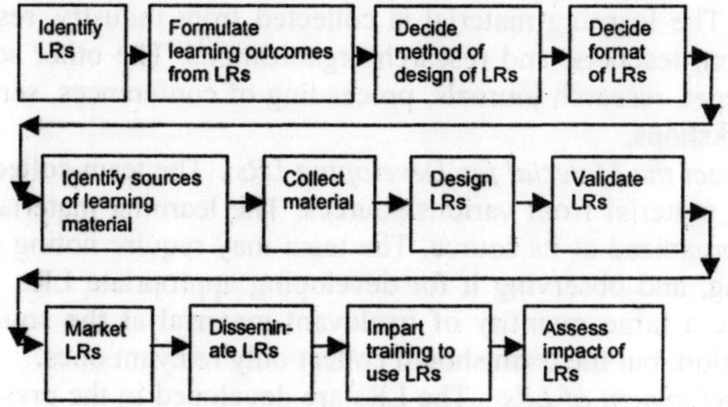

Fig. 8.3 : Design of Learning Resources

Identify the LRs : The LRs to be developed are identified from the curriculum document, hierarchy of implementation plans and learning process. The existing resources available in market are being used in institutions and also a good source for identifying the LRs. The existing LRs may not be aligned to curriculum requirements so they should not be used directly. Existing LRs should be refined, modified and changed to suit to requirements of curriculum.

Formulate Learning Outcomes of LRs : The learning outcomes of LRs are formulated and stated on the LRs for easy identification and use. The learning outcomes should be specific and guide the users to select and use for developing competency. All the LRs should focus on the learning of students and not on the teaching.

Decide the Method of Design: The LRs are designed in a systematic way to assure quality of learning, effectiveness, efficiency, and economy. The LRDC should design a standard procedure for producing different LRs. This process avoids *ad hoc* and personalized decisions to develop the LRs. This process is used by all the teams to maintain uniformity. It prevents the waste of time, money, efforts and physical resources.

Decide Format of LRs : The well-designed format of LRs helps the team to visualize the output of its efforts and align the efforts accordingly. In fact, the format of LRs gives a holistic view of the LRs to developers, users and evaluators. The LRs can be easily categorized and organized. The points for design of LRs are stated in different types of LRs.

Identify the Sources of Learning Material : The team should identify the sources of information for developing the LRs. The curriculum design team is a big source to provide information related to LRs. The learning material is collected from industry, resource institution, teachers, and research organizations. The other sources are internet, research journals, proceeding of conferences, seminars and workshops.

Collect the Material for Developing LRs : The team collects the learning material from various sources. The learning material may not be organized at its source. The team may require noting down, recording, and observing it for developing appropriate LRs. There could be a large quantity of irrelevant material at the source of information, but the team should collect only relevant ones.

Development of LRs : The LRs are developed in the prescribed format. The team organizes the learning material observing the principles of learning, education technology and education psychology. It arranges the learning material logically to develop the competency. One dedicated team should develop all the LRs for achieving one competency to maintain unity, relevance, effectiveness, efficiency and continuity. It helps to prevent duplication, gaps and overlaps of information. The LRs contain visuals, diagrams, photographs, exhibits, flow charts, relation diagram etc. to make them interesting and attractive. The assessment of the progress of learning and rewards for achievement should be in-built in the LRs.

Validate the LRs : The draft of the LRs is validated by a larger team of teachers, students and LR development experts. Generally, the validation team is different than development team. It validates the LRs using criteria such as alignment to competency, suiting to the entry behaviour of students, attractiveness, accuracy of content, logic and sequence, promote involvement of students, stimulate thinking, and so on. If possible, try out and refine it on the basis of comments, suggestions and feedback.

Market the LRs : The LRDC designs and implements the marketing strategies to market the LRs to institutions, industries, and society. The LRs will be useful to them for various purposes such as conducting continuing education, distance education and e-learning programmes, creating awareness on particular technology or habits or practices.

Disseminate the LRs : The LRDC disseminates the LRs to institutions, industries and other organization. If necessary, it organizes training programmes for teachers to use the LRs to make the learning process joyful, effective and efficient.

Assess the Impact of LRs : The LRDC designs a mechanism to collect the feedback on criteria such as format of LRs, quality, effectiveness, time consumed, interest shown by students, difficulty in use, administering problems, cost of LRs, etc. It also assesses the impact of LRs on achievement of learning objectives or development of competencies. It invites suggestions of the teachers, students and experts to add value to LRs in next cycle.

6. Learning Resource Bank

The learning resource bank is a concept which can be taken up by the LRDC on the concept of build, operate and transfer (BOT) basis. According to the need LRs can be added or removed from the bank.

The LRs can be banked in soft or hard copies. The teachers and students can draw the resources as and when they want to use it. The LRDC should not only develop the LRs, but should also invite several teachers, resource persons, industry persons and students to contribute their unique experiences and new initiatives taken by them to the learning resource bank to bring positive changes. The LRs bank should maintain account of all types of resources such as various learning methods as LRs, experiences of conducting learning methods and assessment tools. The LRs bank should compile unique outputs of the learning process. The LRs bank should function effectively and efficiently to support the learning of teachers as well as students.

7. Guidelines for Developing Learning Resources

The LRDC plays a very important role in making the learning process successful. In absence of LRs teachers will practice old methods of teaching learning. They will justify that they are interested in teaching learning but they do not get sufficient time or resources to complete the curriculum. They will also have excuses of not having the LRs when caught unaware about latest methods and LRs and using traditional methods of instruction. To ensure effective and efficient implementation of curriculum the following guidelines are observed for design and development of LRs :

- Formulate a policy to implement curriculum and use LRs in all institutions for all the disciplines.
- Develop curriculum document and LRs at a central place in the country/state. Different centres of excellence in the country can be assigned the work of curriculum and LRs development in different disciplines.
- Establish strong linkages with industry, research institutions, centre of excellences, engineering institutions and sign memorandum of association for collaborative working.
- Design and develop a scientific and detailed curriculum document.
- Identify all types of LRs from curriculum document and try to explore alternatives.
- Prepare a plan to develop LRs in shortest possible time. Obviously, for the first time it may take longer time but in next cycle it will take comparatively less time.

- Train the resource persons to design and develop LRs applying principles of learning, education psychology, education technology, education research, and information communication technology.
- Develop standard processes for design and development of various types of LRs to assure quality at every stage.
- Design standard formats for different types of LRs to organize the learning material in a particular pattern.
- Facilitate and support the learning material collection process from the industry.
- Design and validate the LRs and if possible try out for its relevance and effectiveness. Ensure the use of principles of learning, communication, assessment and feedback in the final output of LRs.
- Check the quality of LRs against the criteria discussed in this chapter.
- Classify and store it for effective dissemination.
- Refine, add value and re-engineer the LRs on the basis of the feedback.

8. Training of LRs Development Team

The LRs development team should professionally work to effectively and efficiently produce the LRs. The team of resource persons should be trained in topics such as types and purpose of LRs, method of design of specific type of LRs, hardware and software requirements, use of software for designing LRs, organization of learning material in LRs, format of LRs, principles of learning, and assessment of learning.

9. Learning Resources Utilization Centre (LRUC)

The higher learning institutions should create well-equipped Learning Resources Utilization Centres (LRUCs) to purchase, store and use LRs. The LRUC facilitates the enrichment of learning process. The LRUC is based on the concept, principles and assumptions of learning, such as each student has unique style of learning, individual students learn on their own pace, learn in natural and self-controlled learning environment, learn when they are accountable for learning, learn to pursue their ambitions/vision/hobby, learn interacting with peers and environment in open and free environment, learn when reach and meaningful learning experiences are provided, the learning is effective when students use all senses for learning and stimulus is changed and so on. The LRUC fulfils the learning requirements of students. It promotes use of student centred innovative methods of learning. It helps teachers to inculcate self-learning and student centre learning environment and discard traditional teaching methods. The habit of self-learning in students enables them to cope up with technological changes.

The LRUC should encourage learning at any time. The LRUC should be open for more than 12 hours in a day and holidays to facilitate student-centred learning methods in the institution. It should be continuously updated and catalogue of LRs should be easily available to the students. The LRs should be accessible to students without any barrier. The LRUC should be user friendly. The students should be educated to operate hardware and software in the LRUC. It should have connectivity and accessibility to all LRs available in the world. It should enable the teachers and students to participate in video conferencing and other significant learning events. The teachers should promote use of LRs using various techniques such as giving assignments, projects and problems to students based on LRs.

Apart from the LRUC, laboratories, workshops and exhibition room should be stocked with LRs. Classrooms should be equipped with media ready for use by teachers and students. The classrooms and laboratories should support use of variety of learning methods and learning settings. The industry is a great storehouse of resources and can also function as a LRUC. The teachers should plan industrial visits and industrial training of students for a longer duration without worrying much about the theory.

10. Criteria for Selecting LRs

The higher education programmes are being offered for the last several decades and quite a good range and number of LRs have been developed by various organizations, institutions, and resource centres. These LRs can also be selected and used by teachers. These resources can be refined to tune to the requirements of the development of competency in the students. The LRs are designed/selected considering variety and number of factors such as alignment to achieve learning objectives and competency, time required and saved in comparison to conventional resources, effectiveness and efficiency for learning, match with entry behaviour of the students, flexibility in using, relevant to current practices in world of work, completeness, production cost, cost of using, ease of use, time and efforts required to develop or procure, maintenance and handling cost, and development of competencies.

11. Audit the Learning Resources

The LRs are designed by LRDC and used by teachers working in thousands of institutions across the country. The teaching learning process is supplemented and complemented by LRs. The effective and efficient design and use of LRs may prevent problems related to teaching learning and assure quality of learning to a great extent in achieving learning objectives professionally. The share of use of LRs in higher education may be more than 50 per cent with respect to time available for teaching learning process. Therefore, it becomes imperative to audit the process of developing the LRs, their quality and use. The audit of all the LRs is conducted on objective criteria stated in Format 8.1. The LRDC conducts the audit of process of developing the LRs and quality of LRs. Teachers working in individual institutions conduct the audit of use of LRs. The LRDC may conduct formal in-depth audit of all the LRs after every five years and informal fast track audit every year. The teachers may conduct informal audit of each type of LRs after every semester and improve the use of LRs in next cycle.

12. Conclusion

The LRs enrich the learning process in higher learning institutions and save time, effort and material to develop the competency in all the students. They are useful to change the stimulus and change the mood of the students. The beauty of the LRs is that they develop the associated competencies without any additional efforts of the teachers. The LRDC scientifically and systematically develops the LRs at a centralized place. The LRs are developed in LRDC by a team of experts drawn from related fields. The team observes the requirements of the competency, entry behaviour of the students, learning styles, learning modes of the students and design the LRs. The learning material is collected from the industry, research institutions and centres of excellence to design the LRs. The LRDC networks with the organizations and collaborates for developing, documenting and capturing the industrial practices. The LRDC develops and distributes the LRs to the institutions. It imparts training to teachers for using LRs in teaching learning process. It adds value to the LRs through conducting research studies and receiving feedback from the users.

13. Format

Audit the LRs

Instructions for Auditors: The LRs are audited on the criteria stated in Format 8.1 given below. During the audit of LRs, if you come across deficiencies/gaps/weaknesses, note down the extent of the gap in column 3 and description of the gaps in column 4 of the format. After examining the complete LR against each criteria and noting down the deficiencies/gaps/weaknesses, think about the strategies to bring improvement in the LRs and note it down in column 5. You can think about value additions with respect to criteria under consideration even if you do not find any weaknesses, mention it in column 5. Please use following scale for indicating the extent of deficiencies/gaps/weaknesses, in column 3. If you find that a particular criterion is not applicable for auditing the given LR you can leave that row blank.

- 5 – indicates very high deficiency/gap/weakness,
- 4 – indicates high deficiency/gap/weakness,
- 3 – indicates medium deficiency/gap/weakness,
- 2 – indicates low deficiency/gap/weakness,
- 1 – indicates very low deficiency/gap/weakness, and
- 0 – indicates no deficiency/gap/weakness.

Format 8.1 : Audit—The Learning Resources

Sl. No.	Criteria	Extent of Gaps	Description of Gaps or scope for improvement	Strategies to bring improvement
1	2	3	4	5
A.	**Process of development**			
1.	Based on curriculum, instructional strategy and learning requirements			

Format 8.1 : *Contd.*

Sl. No.	*Criteria*	*Extent of Gaps*	*Description of Gaps or scope for improvement*	*Strategies to bring improvement*
1	2	3	4	5
2.	Use of real life practices			
3.	Based on principle of learning and learning style of students			
4.	Free from duplication of information, investment, time and efforts in development			
5.	Use of latest software in development			
6.	Provision for validation and tryout			
7.	Economic in production, storage, maintenance and distribution			
B.	Quality of LRs			
8.	Aligned to learning objectives and competency			
9.	Suitability for developing associated competency along with core competency			
10.	Precise, concise, complete, self explanatory, attractive, interesting, legible, accurate in information, logical, sequential, and relevant to current practices			
11.	Benchmarked with the best			
12.	Variety in range			
13.	Create opportunities to apply previous learning, explore the unknown, and experience the truth			
14.	Create interest, curiosity, and challenges for learning			
15.	Assure quality in learning			
16.	Technically, psychologically and financially feasible			
17.	Creative and different			

Format 8.1 : *Contd.*

Sl. No.	*Criteria*	*Extent of Gaps*	*Description of Gaps or scope for improvement*	*Strategies to bring improvement*
1	2	3	4	5
18.	**Based on real life situations**			
19.	**Maintain uniformity and continuity in learning process**			
20	**In-built assessment and reward mechanism**			
21.	**Matches with entry behaviour, learning style, learning mode, learning mood of students**			
22.	**Handy to carry and use**			
23.	**Guidelines are mentioned for teachers and students for conducting teaching learning process**			
C.	**Use of LRs**			
24.	**Availability of physical resources, hardware and sitting arrangement required**			
25.	**Promote involvement of students**			
26.	**Create joyful learning**			
27.	**Prevent waste of time, money and efforts in use**			
28.	**Save time and effort for teaching as well as learning**			
29.	**Reduce dependence for learning on teachers**			
30.	**Empower students for learning**			
31.	**Provide diversity and flexibility in approach to learning**			
32.	**Easy to learn**			
33.	**Provide opportunity to use all the senses of learning**			
34.	**Encourage self learning, mutual learning and collaborative learning**			
35.	**Use for assessment and feedback**			

14. Review Questions

1. Define learning resources.
2. State the purposes of using learning resources in teaching learning process.
3. List classification of learning resources.
4. State the benefits of learning resources designed on learning methods.
5. State the types of learning assignments.
6. Compare the strengths and limitations of different types of assignments.
7. State advantages of learning media.
8. Describe the functions of the learning resources development centre.
9. State the composition of learning resources development centre.
10. Describe process of developing learning resources.
11. Explain the concept of learning resources bank.
12. List the guidelines for developing learning resources.
13. State the training areas of learning resources development team.
14. State the concept of learning resources utilization centre.
15. Describe the functions of the learning resources utilization centre.
16. State the criteria for selecting learning resources for assuring learning.
17. List the criteria for auditing the learning resources.

15. Activities for Auditors

Activity 8.1: Develop different types of learning resources.
Activity 8.2: Audit different types of learning resources.

9

Audit—The Performance Appraisal System

ADVANCE ORGANIZER

Scientifically and participatively designed performance appraisal system can assure effective and efficient performance of faculty and staff members in core areas of performance of the institution. The concept of performance appraisal evolved over the years in corporate sector. This concept can be adopted for educational institutions. On one hand, the performance appraisal for faculty and staff members is integrated with the vision, missions, goals, strategic plans, perspective plans and annual plans of the institution. And on the other hand, it emphasizes the use of capabilities, capacities, strengths of individuals and teams for achieving excellence in performance. The emerging concepts of performance appraisal, current status, trends in performance appraisal, and audit of performance appraisal is precisely discussed in this chapter. Two types of Formats are recommended for auditing the performance appraisal system of educational institutions. Format 9.1 is used to audit the process of performance appraisal system development and Format 9.2 is used to audit the performance appraisal system, its implementation and improvement.

1. Rationale

The faculty members play a vital role in shaping the future of the students. They are the key persons to develop basic competencies in the students on which technical, professional, and social competencies are developed. They prepare the foundation for developing life skills in the students. They prepare the students to develop professional and higher order competencies in joyful way. The generic skills such as learning to learn, thinking to think, joyful learning, creative and analytical skills, values, ethics, moral, self-evaluation and reflection, positive attitude towards life etc. take shape in educational institutions.

The various stakeholders have variety of expectations from faculty members. The role of faculty members is designed considering the expectations of stakeholders. They are prepared and developed to perform the role professionally to satisfy the expectations of stakeholders in order to build the academic image of the self and their institution in society.

The National Policy on Education–1986 has given considerable stress on improving quality of education. It considers the teachers as the pivot of the education system. The teachers have to perform multiple roles such as teaching, research, consultancy, development of instructional resources, administration, student services, acquisition and development of expertise in their chosen field of specialization, and extension. In order to promote the excellence in education, the National Policy on Education recognizes the need to perform such multiple roles by teachers. The National Policy on Education also stipulates the introduction of performance appraisal system for teachers, which will make the teachers accountable for their work. It states that a system of teachers' evaluation should be open, participative, and data based. It should create reasonable opportunities of promotion to higher grades.

The academic performance of educational institutions depends on the performance of the faculty members and other significant members involved in carrying out the academic business. Especially faculty members are considered to be the backbone of the academic activities. Their performance is crucial to shape the behaviour of the students. The performance of faculty members should be planned, monitored and measured to ascertain the quality of education. Looking to the changing scenario of education the concept of developing lifelong learning is becoming important in educational institutions.

The faculty members have been traditionally discharging their duties and responsibilities for a long time. The University Grants Commission, All India Council for Technical Education, National Council of Education, Research and Training, Central Government, State Governments, and Society of the educational institutions have suggested the role for faculty and staff members. This role is indicative and may not be complete looking to the specific requirements of different educational institutions. It happens because different institutions are having their own vision, mission, and goals that may require its members to perform variety of roles. The expectations of students and their parents are increasing and expanding everyday so there may be continuous change in the roles of the faculty and staff members. Number of processes take place in different areas of functioning of educational institutions to accomplish the vision and mission. It is not necessary that all faculty and staff members perform all the roles prescribed by statutory body equally. Teams' structure is becoming important in contemporary time rather than working individually. There is a need to derive the role of different position holders as well as teams keeping in view the roles prescribed by statutory body, stakeholders' expectations, institutional requirements and individual requirements. Role so derived should be appropriately allocated to the individual teachers and teams according to their competencies, capabilities, experience and willingness. Individuals and teams' performance should be measured on goals or objectives set by them against these roles.

The performance appraisal system followed in educational institutions is not based on scientific methods of planning, implementation of plans, monitoring and evaluation. Now variety of performance appraisal models, based on scientific principles are available and in use. These models can be adopted and used in educational institutions. There is a need of the system that continuously monitors the progress of performance qualitatively and quantitatively. This is necessary for the growth and development of the faculty members and at the same time for achieving the excellence. The growth and development of faculty members is possible in the appraisal situation where progress is monitored and underlying causes are identified for the poor performance or excellent performance. These causes are used to design the strategies to improve the performance of individuals and teams. Individuals and teams constantly innovate methods for improving the performance.

2. Emerging Concepts of Performance Appraisal

The concept of performance appraisal has been used for a long time in various forms. Its concept and purposes changed time to time. The authors propose following concepts for educational institutions:

- It is an instrument of assessing the performance of individuals and teams and to take decisions to enhance their effectiveness and efficiency within current environment and available resources.

- It is a system derived on the basis of strategic, perspective and tactical plan of the institution to develop the capacity and capability of faculty members to implement the institution plans to achieve the vision, missions, goals and objectives.
- It is a tool to give rewards and create opportunities for the faculty and staff members to develop themselves to their full potential.
- It is a system to define the scope of the work in terms of roles and responsibilities of faculty and staff members and develop them to perform professionally.
- It is a tool for deciding and organizing faculty and staff development programmes and creating attractive rewards for well performers.
- It is a proactive process of planning the performance and performing to achieve the challenging objectives.
- It is a process of learning from feedback of the self and stakeholders on the quality of performance with an objective to improve performance.
- It is a process of creating and grabbing opportunities for professional development of faculty and staff members.
- It is a process of mutual, collaborative, cooperative and action learning in which all the faculty and staff members participate with positive attitude to learn and enhance the academic climate of the institution, to face the academic challenges and competitions.
- It is a prerequisite process performed by the institution that becomes base for taking significant decisions such as training, counselling, guidance, and coaching of individuals and teams.

3. Current Status of Performance Appraisal System

The performance appraisal system for educational institutions is not scientifically designed and implemented because lack of awareness and less accountability at all levels. In fact, the complete planning approach including performance planning is missing in most of the educational institutions. In the absence of performance appraisal system the faculty and staff members perform conventionally and traditionally. Their performance is casually assessed. There is no system for performance planning except preparing time table for conducting theory and practical classes traditionally. The performance is not much directly linked with recognition, rewards, incentives and development opportunities. The performance assessment is totally based on reactive and problem solving approach. The concept of professional management of educational institutions is missing and so as the performance appraisal. One of the significant causes for this may be poor salary and incentive structure in educational institutions in comparison to corporate world.

4. Trends in Performance Appraisal

In last two decades, numbers of models of performance appraisal have been developed and implemented in corporate sector. These models were refined based on experiences. The experts have focused more on quality of performance rather than quantitative performance. Some centres of excellence in education sector also used the experiences of corporate sector to design their performance appraisal system and implemented it. It resulted in brand image of the institutions. The main features of the performance appraisal system are participatively and scientifically designed, focus on planning in core performance areas, improvement and development, integrated with vision and mission of the institution, objective and data based, emphasis on self evaluation and feedback, informal approach in contrast to formal approach, 360 degree appraisal for mutual feedback, performance linked to training, incentives and rewards.

The performance of individuals and teams is integrated with strategic, perspective and annual plan of the institution and it is the base for designing the performance appraisal system for any institution. Gupta (2008) proposed a self-explanatory model shown in Fig. 9.1 that indicates links between various components of planning from institution level to individual level. The institutions intending to design and implement performance appraisal system for the first time use research approach to design and implement the performance appraisal system. They design the research instruments based on the strategic plan of the institution, core areas of performance, curricular and co-curricular requirements, statutory requirements, present as well as future expected roles and responsibilities of faculty and staff members, expectations of internal as well as external stakeholders, personal aspirations and ambitions of individuals. They design different instruments for different position holders and their respective stakeholders. These instruments are tried out and refined on the basis of results of try out. Then these instruments are administered on larger population to collect information on quantitative and qualitative parameters of performance. The information is classified and analysed to design the formats for performance appraisal. These formats are circulated to appraisers and appraisees for comments. The formats are further refined based on the comments and used for performance appraisal. Generally performance appraisal manual is prepared by institutions to systematically implement the performance appraisal system.

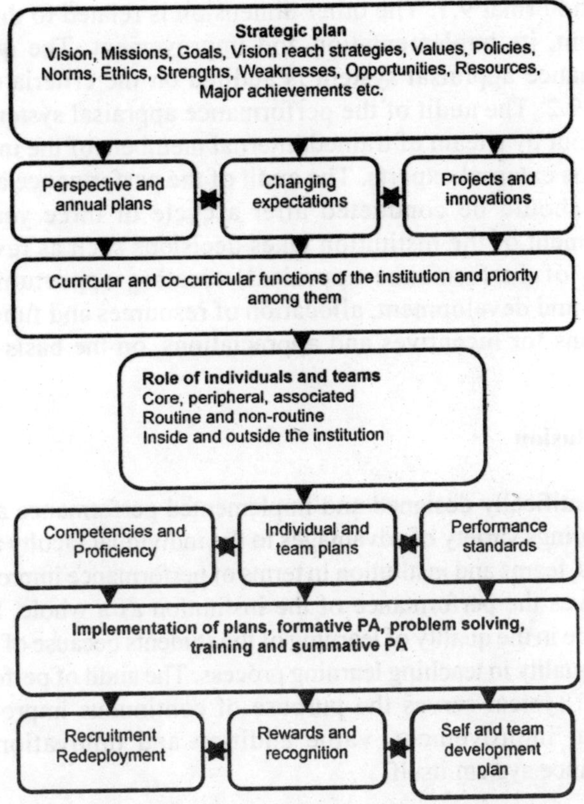

Fig. 9.1: Base for Performance Appraisal

5. Performance Appraisal System Audit

The audit of performance appraisal system is conducted to assess the effectiveness of current performance appraisal system, refine it in the light of current and future requirements and educate the faculty and staff members to implement the refined performance appraisal system. The performance appraisal system audit can be conducted on two dimensions. One dimension is related to the process of developing the performance appraisal system. The scientifically developed performance appraisal system seeks the commitment of the teachers for accepting the system. The process of developing the performance appraisal is audited on the criteria stated in Format 9.1. The other dimension is related to the quality of system, its implementation and improvement. The quality of performance appraisal system is audited on the criteria stated in Format 9.2. The audit of the performance appraisal system can be carried out by a team of trained internal members of the institution as well as external experts. The audit of the performance appraisal system should be conducted after a cycle of three years. The management of the institution takes decisions such as revision of formats of performance appraisal, creating opportunities for training and development, allocation of resources and funds, more provisions for incentives and appreciations, on the basis of audit results.

6. Conclusion

The scientifically designed and implemented performance appraisal system brings variety of advantages to the individual faculty and staff members, teams and institution in terms of performance improvement. It improves the performance of the institution as a whole. It brings excellence in the quality of learning of the students because of inherent in-built quality in teaching learning process. The audit of performance appraisal system serves the purpose of continuous improvement, continual improvement, value addition and innovation in the performance system itself.

7. Format

Audit the Process of Performance Appraisal System Development

Instructions for Auditors : The process of developing the performance appraisal is audited on the criteria stated in Format 9.1. During the audit of the process of development of the performance appraisal system if you come across deficiencies/gaps/weaknesses, note down the extent of the gap in column 3 and description of the gaps in column 4 of the format. After examining the complete process of developing the performance appraisal against each criteria and noting down the deficiencies/gaps/weaknesses, think about the strategies to bring improvement in the performance appraisal system and note it down in column 5. You can think about value addition with respect to criteria under consideration even if you do not find any weaknesses, and mention it in column 5. Please use following scale for indicating the extent of deficiencies/gaps/weaknesses in column 3.

- 5 – indicates very high deficiency/gap/weakness,
- 4 – indicates high deficiency/gap/weakness,
- 3 – indicates medium deficiency/gap/weakness,
- 2 – indicates low deficiency/gap/weakness,
- 1 – indicates very low deficiency/gap/weakness, and
- 0 – indicates no deficiency/gap/weakness.

Format 9.1 : Audit—The Process of Performance Appraisal System Development

Sl. No.	*Criteria*	*Extent of Gaps*	*Description of Gaps or scope for improvement*	*Strategies to bring improvement*
1	*2*	*3*	*4*	*5*
1.	Participatively designed involving apraisee and appraisers			
2.	Used significant, direct and strong indicators of performance in core areas of performance			
3.	Quantitative as well as qualitative parameters are considered			
4.	Designed under the guidance of experts			
5.	Designed holistically			
6.	Considers the capacity and capability of faculty and staff members			

Format 9.1 : *Contd.*

Sl. No.	*Criteria*	*Extent of Gaps*	*Description of Gaps or scope for improvement*	*Strategies to bring improvement*
1	*2*	*3*	*4*	*5*
7.	Integrated with institutional planning			
8.	Takes into account the limitations of the resources			
9.	Alternatives for appraising the performance are considered			
10.	Duplication, redundancy and ineffective elements are removed			
11.	Validated by implementers			

Audit the Performance Appraisal System, its Implementation, Evaluation and Improvement

Instructions for Auditors : Audit the performance appraisal system, its implementation and improvement on the criteria stated in the Format 9.2. During the audit of performance appraisal system, if you come across deficiencies/gaps/weaknesses, note down the extent of gap in column 3 and description of the gap in column 4 of the format. After auditing the performance appraisal system against each criteria and noting down the deficiencies/gaps/weaknesses think about the improvements in performance appraisal system in the light of various criteria and note it down in column 5. You can think about value additions with respect to the criteria under consideration even if you do not find any weakness, and mention it in column 5. Please use the following scale for indicating extent of deficiencies/gaps/weaknesses in column 3.

- 5 – indicates very high deficiency/gap/weakness,
- 4 – indicates high deficiency/gap/weakness,
- 3 – indicates medium deficiency/gap/weakness,
- 2 – indicates low deficiency/gap/weakness,
- 1 – indicates very low deficiency/gap/weakness, and
- 0 – indicates no deficiency/gap/weakness.

Format 9.2 : Audit—The Performance Appraisal System, its Implementation and Improvement

Sl. No.	*Criteria*	*Extent of Gaps*	*Description of Gaps or scope for improvement*	*Strategies to bring improvement*
1	2	3	4	5
A.	Design of the performance appraisal system			
1.	Does it serve following purposes at institutional level : • Growth and development of institution • Effective planning of performance of individuals and teams • Benchmarking of performance • Human resources development • Effective deployment of human resources • Documentation of performance • Decisions on rewards and incentives • Decide authority, responsibility and accountability • Identifying training and development needs and preparing employee development plans • Deployment and redeployment of individuals • Succession planning • Mutually beneficial to employees			
2.	Does it serve following purposes at individual level : • Exploring potential of individuals • Self-development • Time management			

Format 9.2 : *Contd.*

Sl. No.	*Criteria*	*Extent of Gaps*	*Description of Gaps or scope for improvement*	*Strategies to bring improvement*
1	2	3	4	5
	• Empowering individuals			
	• Creating healthy relationship			
	• Opportunities for learning through feedback, guidance, counselling and mentoring			
	• Self-satisfaction			
3.	Does it satisfy following characteristics :			
	• Promotes performance planning at the beginning of the semester			
	• Transparent based on data, facts and figures			
	• Task oriented			
	• Development oriented			
	• Formative and summative			
	• Formal and informal			
	• Constructive and productive			
	• Less emotional			
	• Emphasize on self-development			
	• Appraisal by self and all other significant stakeholders including students			
	• Scientific use of teaching learning methods and media			
	• Acceptable to all the members			
	• Less time consuming			
	• Continually updated			
	• Less paper work			
4.	Does it focus on following :			
	• Creativity and innovation			
	• Change and development			

Format 9.2 : *Contd.*

Sl. No.	*Criteria*	*Extent of Gaps*	*Description of Gaps or scope for improvement*	*Strategies to bring improvement*
1	2	3	4	5
	• Collaborative learning • Performance problem prevention • Joyful learning • Rewards, growth and development • Autonomy with accountability • Effective communication • Career development • Mutual trust between the appraiser and appraisee • Improvement in present as well as future performance • Promote self discipline			
5.	Are the formats of performance appraisal : • Comprehensive but precise • Relevant • Promote effective planning simple to understand and interpret • Focus on quantitative as well as qualitative performance • Measures end results as well as process effectiveness • Related to stake of the appraiser • Facilitate monitoring and review of the performance • Benchmark performance • Linked to rewards, incentives and development			
6.	Performance appraisal manual prepared on the following points : • Objectives of performance appraisal			

Format 9.2 : *Contd.*

Sl. No.	*Criteria*	*Extent of Gaps*	*Description of Gaps or scope for improvement*	*Strategies to bring improvement*
1	2	3	4	5
	• Key areas of performance • Roles, responsibility, authority and accountability of different position holders • Formats of performance appraisal for appraisees and appraisers • Code of conduct to be observed during performance appraisal • Criteria for interpretation of performance results • Appreciation, rewards and incentives for excellent performance • Grievance handling mechanism			
B.	**Performance appraisal implementation**			
7.	Awareness and education of institutional members on performance appraisal and their consensus on it			
8.	Institutional, department and individual planning workshops conducted and plans validated by related persons			
9.	Commitment of the management to provide resources to implement the plans			
10.	Training of appraisees and appraisers for organizing appraisal sessions			
11.	Training and development opportunities are created for employees to achieve excellence			
12.	Support, help and guidance provided during performance			

Format 9.2 : *Contd.*

Sl. No.	*Criteria*	*Extent of Gaps*	*Description of Gaps or scope for improvement*	*Strategies to bring improvement*
1	2	3	4	5
13.	Formative appraisal is conducted by self and related persons informally, and constructive feedback is offered for improvement			
14.	Evidences maintained by appraisees related to achievements			
15.	Free from appraisal errors			
16.	Summative appraisal is conducted in conducive and encouraging environment maintaining transparency and objectivity			
17.	Analysis of performance to recognize achievements and reward them			
18.	Report on results of performance appraisal			
C.	**Performance improvement**			
19.	Collective learning through experience sharing related to performance appraisal system implementation using variety of approaches such as meetings, workshops, interaction sessions, creativity sessions, case studies of critical situations Inputs to next year performance planning			
20.	Guidance, counselling, coaching and mentoring for improvement in performance			
21.	Training and development opportunities such as action learning, role play, problem based learning, conferences, seminars, panel discussions, quality circles, self-learning etc.			
22.	Identifying and removing the gaps in performance appraisal system			

Format 9.2 : *Contd.*

Sl. No.	*Criteria*	*Extent of Gaps*	*Description of Gaps or scope for improvement*	*Strategies to bring improvement*
1	2	3	4	5
23.	Value addition in teaching learning process			
24.	Refinement of performance appraisal system			

8. Review Questions

1. Define the concept of performance appraisal.
2. State the provisions made in National Policy on Education about performance appraisal.
3. Compare various definition of performance appraisal and formulate your own definition.
4. Describe the base for designing performance appraisal system for educational institutions.
5. Explain the relationship between performance appraisal and rewards.
6. Describe the types of performance appraisal.
7. List the criteria for appraising the performance of faculty members.
8. State the characteristics of performance appraisal system.
9. Explain the concept of 360 degree appraisal.

9. Activities for Auditors

Activity 9.1: Design the performance appraisal system for one educational institution.
Activity 9.2: Design the performance appraisal manual for one educational institution.
Activity 9.3: Design formats of performance appraisal for faculty members.
Activity 9.4: Conduct audit of performance appraisal system of one educational institution.

A Case Study on "Introducing Academic Audit in Technical Institutions"

The National Institute of Technical Teachers' and Research conducted a three-day workshop on quality of education. This workshop was attended by 40 Directors and Principals of Government and Government aided institutions. In this workshop recent concepts related to quality of education were discussed and debated. These concepts have improved the quality in manufacturing and service industries. In education, these concepts are being used for developing learning to learn and learning for life skills in the students to enhance their learning maturity level. It is also highlighted that the learning should be joyful and harness the potential of the students for their career. The technical institutions should implement competency-based curriculum, outcome based curriculum, problem based curriculum etc. in modular and flexible mode to make the learning purposeful. It is also discussed that the elements of TQM such as quality vision, quality policy, scientifically designed systems, continuous improvement, value addition, quality assurance, teaming with customers, etc. should be used in technical institutions.

The participants of the workshop pointed out that quality should be assured by design and not by chance. They discussed the current procedure of NBA accreditation and concluded that this procedure does not compel institutions to assure quality but it promotes quality control. The institutions performing well by chance get accreditation. The consistency in performance may be questioned in such cases. It does not satisfy the specific needs of the institution as well as programme. The NBA accreditation is done against national criteria that may not be relevant in local or specific context. The participants debated on the concept of quality assurance and concluded that the technical institutions should design quality systems at institutional level for all academic purposes. They decided that the quality system should also be aligned to their vision and mission statement. The system should be designed observing the principles of education management, education technology and education psychology.

The Directors, professors and principals also discussed the process of designing, implementing and evaluating the academic systems. They highlighted on designing the core academic processes using information technology. They considered the options of using alternative teaching learning methods and learning resources. They have pointed out shortage of competent faculty and modern resources. But these problems are resolved by generating alternatives. Deploy and redeploy faculty members for various short-term academic purposes, developing them through training, guiding and counselling. Engage retired faculty members and persons from industry to fill up the gap of shortage of staff. So far the physical resources is concerned it is also decided that the institutions cannot develop all types of resources so the concept of sharing, networking and collaborating with industry, sister institutions and resource institutions should be used.

It is pointed out by a few principals that many students are joining the engineering programmes from rural areas with low entry behaviour so it is very difficult and rather it is a challenge for the institutions to provide quality education to them. The issue is discussed and resolved that the institutions should offer some bridge courses such as, personality development programmes, communication skills development programmes etc. to raise their level at par with others and then start teaching regular programmes in which they are admitted.

The participants appreciated the efforts made by the professors to make the workshop successful and fruitful to them. They thanked the professors for not delivering the long lectures and concentrating discussion on main issues related to quality. They also thanked professors for providing them opportunities for open and creative discussions.

Dr. B. L. Gupta is a Principal of Autonomous Polytechnic, Sengabad. He is Ph.D. in industrial engineering and has 10 years' experience in industry and 15 years' experience in technical education. He is impressed with the concept of quality assurance in technical education and academic audit. He decided to implement the quality assurance system in his institution. He called a meeting of all the HODs and made a presentation on outcomes of the workshop he attended. After that he expressed his interest to implement the academic audit system in the institution. He invited suggestions and comments of the HODs on his decision. The HODs responded that let them study the concepts and modalities and after that they will offer the comments. The principal appointed one senior most HOD Prof. Ragade as a coordinator who is going to retire after 2 years. The principal handed over the workshop material and copies of the power point presentations to Prof. Ragade and asked him to prepare a detailed action plan to implement the academic audit system in the institution.

Prof. Ragade thought that all the programmes of the institution are accredited by NBA for five years, it means the institution is providing quality education and there is no need to work on so many systems because the institution is implementing performance appraisal system as well. He did not take any action on the request of the principal for a month. After one month, principal Gupta asked Prof. Ragade about the action plan. Ragade replied that he was busy in examination work as he is the examination superintendent. He promised the principal to prepare it after completion of examination. Meanwhile Mr. Ragade contacted nearby autonomous polytechnic and asked about the implementation of academic audit at their institution. He was told by the principal polytechnic that he is not aware about the concept but he has appointed a consultant to prepare documents for obtaining ISO certificates. The principal of this polytechnic informed Ragade about the advantages of ISO certified institution.

Ragade prepared a note for his principal that academic audit is an excellent concept for quality education. It is the need of the day. The institution should implement the concept under the guidance of NITTTR where the principal has attended the training. He proposed in the note that the consultant should develop the academic audit system for them and the institution will implement it under the guidance of consultant. Principal agreed to the proposal of Ragade and requested NITTTR to design the academic audit system for them. The NITTTR replied that they do not develop the system but they help the institutions to develop the system on their own.

Again Gupta asked Ragade to take actions on designing and implementing academic audit system. Ragade designed the formats to monitor the progress and quality of performance of faculty and staff members. It was based on current performance appraisal system of the institution, literature provided by NITTTR and NBA accreditation manual. He designed the formats for all incharges, HODs, TPO, Workshop superintendent, Librarian, senior and selection grade lecturers and lecturers. Theses formats were submitted to the principal and it was requested to assure, whether the faculty and staff members are progressing well and performing better. Mr. Ragade suggested that principal can only assess the quality by audit of the performance of all the concerned persons every three months. Principal agreed to the proposal of Ragade and informed all the concerned persons through circular that he is going to audit the performance of every teacher in the first week of the month. He further directed all the concerned persons that they should fill up the prescribed proforma and keep it ready when they are called for audit. The proforma were enclosed with circular.

The day people received the circular, started criticizing it, informally with their colleagues. Some of them also discussed with their HODs. The HODs were also surprised about the sudden decision of the principal. They have also criticized Ragade. Not a single person in the institution appreciated the circular and its purpose. Some of the closed friends convened informal meeting to stop this business. No one dare to talk to principal on this issue including HODs. But everyday there was informal talk on the issue. Their informal comments which were overheard by everyone as follows :

- It will increase the paper work of the institution, hence wastage of paper.
- It will consume more time, which is a waste of time contributing nothing for quality.
- Our programmes are already accredited for five years in such situation what is the need of it?
- How many experiments this institution will do. The performance appraisal is already a failure because no reward policy is there in the institution. The principal never used the performance appraisal record to appreciate the good performers and punish the poor performers. Everybody is equal in this institution.
- In autonomous institution principal can do anything he likes.
- Class three and four employees are doing nothing and enjoying their salary.
- The principal should take more responsibility to achieve quality in education instead of monitoring the progress of the teachers.
- The principal should provide laptops to all faculty members for preparing powerpoints and other instructional material.
- The principal should consult them for any change. The principal should not use autocratic style in the autonomous polytechnics.
- The principal should give more attention on faculty recruitment and modernizing the laboratories instead of doing paper work.

Dr. B.L. Gupta thought that everybody has understood the main purpose, provisions of the circular and method of filling the format. He did not take any feedback on the circular and format. After one and half months, at the beginning he invited HOD and faculty members of electronics department with filled up proforma. The HOD requested all the faculty members to fill up the proforma and submit it by evening so that next day all can meet principal with their progress. All the faculty members filled up the formats and submitted to HOD with some resentment. Next day whole department faculty members contacted principal Gupta. Principal welcomed them and offered tea. He scanned the filled up proforma of all the faculty members of the department and shown his satisfaction. Gupta asked about the next month activities of the department and problems which is replied by HOD. After some discussions on various plans and issues of the institution Gupta requested department to keep it up.

The other departments were tensed because the electronics department completed the proforma and met the principal. The other departments interacted with the members of the electronics department and shared their experiences about the audit. They got the message that it is a mere formality and they should not worry much about it. Almost same thing happened with all the departments of the institution and the first round of the audit was over without any significant opposition and outcome. Principal Gupta handed over the proforma to Ragade for analysing the information and using it for preparing the annual report, students' magazine, progress report and presentations for stakeholders. Principal could find time to conduct such audits twice in a year. At the end of the year, Ragade prepared a brief report on behalf of the principal on the activities performed by various departments. He appreciated significant contributions made by departments and individuals. Principal Gupta made presentation of this report in governing body meeting and in annual function.

Brief

(1) Identify the strengths and weaknesses of Principal Gupta's approach on implementing academic audit system in the polytechnic.

(2) Based on strengths and weaknesses of Gupta's approach, design a strategy to implement academic audit system in your institution.

Activities to be performed by trainees	*Time*
Individual reading and analysis of case study	10 minutes
Discussion in a group	20 minutes
Preparation for presentation	05 minutes
Time for presentation to each group	07 minutes
Summarization by trainer	05 minutes

Instrument for Academic Audit

In the table given below some statements and their responses are given. There may be more than one response(s) relevant for each statement. Kindly rate the responses in the light of the statement using weightage given in the legend below. You can mention any comments, if you think; it is necessary to better describe your response.

Legend: Strongly agree – 3, Agree – 2, Agree to some extent – 1, Not agree - 0

Sl. No.	*Statements*	*Rating*	*Comment, if any*
1.	**The Academic Audit is defined as:**		
(i)	A systematic review of the administrative and financial processes of any Institution.		
(ii)	A systematic review of overall performance of an institution against scientifically designed academic processes.		
(iii)	A review of design of academic systems on inputs, processes and outputs with pre-decided academic standard of quality.		
(iv)	A process to know the standards of acceptance of academics.		
(v)	A process of internalization of the institution's academic quality assurance policies and practices by the faculty and staff members and implementing the same in letter and spirit.		
(vi)	A process of evaluating the academic programmes of any institution.		

Sl. No.	Statements	Rating	Comment, if any
(vii)	A review process of assuring academic quality of students, learning resources and services.		
(viii)	A performance review process, which is exactly similar to the NBA Accreditation process.		
(ix)	A process for testing the effectiveness of quality assurance policies of institution by examining their influences on academic programmes and learning of the students.		
(x)	A process of reviewing the entire educational policy of the institution.		
(xi)	A systematic review of all those processes that are believed to bring improvements in the quality of teaching learning processes.		
(xii)	A process of building quality culture in the institution to achieve the academic excellence.		
(xiii)	An overall assessment of the institution against norms set by NBA.		
(xiv)	A process to review the classroom notes, lab records and attendance records of all the students by concerned faculty and staff.		
(xv)	A process to check as to how an institution takes account of the views of external stakeholders in improving academic performance.		
(xvi)	A process carried out with a purpose to assure the achievement of pre-decided quality goals by the management of the institution.		
(xvii)	Any other		
2.	**Main purpose of conducting academic audit is :**		
(i)	Assure quality in academic performance of the institution.		
(ii)	Bring continuous improvement in the performance of the faculty, staff and institution.		

Sl. No.	Statements	Rating	Comment, if any
(iii)	Add value to academic performance of each of the programme run by the institution.		
(iv)	Recognize the academic standard of institution.		
(v)	Review the performance of the teachers and learning of the students.		
(vi)	Prevent academic problems of the institution at all levels to sustain quality of programmes.		
(vii)	Benchmark the academic results of the students and teaching learning processes of all the disciplines in the institution.		
(viii)	Reduce complaints related to academic performance of Faculty and Staff members.		
(ix)	Set minimum standard of the academic outputs and activities of all educational programmes.		
(x)	Improve academic climate of the institution.		
(xi)	Compare the actual academic achievements of the institution with set goals and objectives.		
(xii)	Adopt the best academic practices in the institution.		
(xiii)	Test the effectiveness of institutional quality assurance policies by examining their influences on academic programmes.		
(xiv)	Introduce planned change for academic excellence in the institution.		
(xv)	Compare the performance of individuals within the institution.		
(xvi)	Promote accountability of faculty and staff for imparting quality education.		
(xvii)	Find out the interaction between the quality assurance policies and the academic activities of the institution.		
(xviii)	Empower faculty and staff members in the academic interest of the institution.		

Sl. No.	Statements	Rating	Comment, if any
(xix)	Market the academic services and products of the institution.		
(xx)	Identify the gaps in planned and conducted activities of academic programme.		
(xxi)	Grade the performance standards of institution and improve it.		
(xxii)	Take corrective actions immediately for sustaining the quality of academic programmes.		
(xxiii)	Reduce waste of efforts, resources and time of faculty and staff.		
(xxiv)	Enrich the learning process and make the learning joyful.		
(xxv)	Empower faculty members, staff members and students for achieving quality objectives.		
(xxvi)	Lead to fulfil shared vision and missions of the institution.		
(xxvii)	Add value to the performance of persons.		
(xxviii)	Bring cooperative and conducive environment		
(xxix)	Any other		
3.	**Characteristic of academic audit are :**		
(i)	Academic audit is conducted against scientifically and systematically designed academic system.		
(ii)	Continuous monitoring of academic performance against qualitative standards.		
(iii)	Focus on the process assessment and improvement.		
(iv)	Participative and interactive.		
(v)	Constructive for assuring and improving the quality of learning.		
(vi)	Proactive approach for assuring quality.		
(vii)	Interaction between institutional policies and academic units.		
(viii)	Transparent-Public announcement of audit reports.		

Sl. No.	*Statements*	*Rating*	*Comment, if any*
(ix)	Audit follow-up and quality enhancement.		
(x)	Much practicable and less emotional.		
(xi)	Question the performance against fundamental academic processes.		
(xii)	Any other		
4.	**What types of academic audit would give effective results :**		
(i)	Fast track.		
(ii)	Indepth.		
(iii)	Conducted by external expert team.		
(iv)	Conducted by a trained team of faculty and staff members.		
(v)	Conducted by self and peers		
(vi)	Conducted by inter-departmental team		
(vii)	Any other.		
5.	**The governing body, management, faculty members, staff members and students might be educated on academic audit by using various modes such as :**		
(i)	Arrange lecture on academic audit followed by discussion.		
(ii)	Provide comprehensive guidelines on academic audit to all faculty and staff members for reading.		
(iii)	Provide self-learning material on academic audit.		
(iv)	Arrange seminar for deliberating the various issues related to quality of learning of the students.		
(v)	Nominate senior faculty for training and he/she should conduct programmes on academic audit in the institution.		
(vi)	Organize training programme on academic audit for all faculty and staff members for conceptual clarity.		

Sl. No.	*Statements*	*Rating*	*Comment, if any*
(vii)	Organize workshop for all the faculty and staff members to develop institution specific quality and academic audit systems.		
(viii)	Directly start conducting academic audit using general formats if available.		
(ix)	Any other.		
6.	**Before starting the academic audit in any institution, the management of the institution should :**		
(i)	Organize workshop involving all individuals in the process of crafting the Vision, Mission and Goals of the Institution.		
(ii)	Provide responsibility to a group and every individual in the institution to design processes.		
(iii)	Formulate policy guidelines to undertake activities of conducting academic audit.		
(iv)	Pressurizes all the individuals to cooperate in starting the academic audit immediately.		
(v)	Introduce the processes gradually in the institution that brings qualitative improvements in standard.		
(vi)	Formulate many groups to design the processes and criteria and assign the task of design of the academic audit system to these groups.		
(vii)	Set the targets and standards of quality for significant processes.		
(viii)	Identify training needs of individuals and groups for designing the academic audit system.		
(ix)	Organise need based training programmes for all the levels before initiating the process of academic audit.		
(x)	Form an academic audit cell in the institution to manage the academic audit activities.		
(xi)	Give responsibility to appropriate individual.		

Sl. No.	Statements	Rating	Comment, if any
(xii)	Accord priority to academic audit related activities.		
(xiii)	Prepare documents and records of the work done in the institution.		
(xiv)	Organize meetings to take stock of audit work progress at fixed intervals		
(xv)	Any other.		
7.	**To conduct formal academic audit, the management of the institution should :**		
(i)	Organize workshop for all the faculty and staff members including management and trustees.		
(ii)	Fix up the responsibility of the concerned Heads of the Departments to see the accomplishment of quality objectives.		
(iii)	Issue an official order to cooperate and accord priority to academic audit activities in the institution.		
(iv)	Declare the plan of action for conducting academic audit.		
(v)	Announce the groups and assign them activities to be carried out with manual/guidelines to proceed.		
(vi)	Distribute the day and date-wise time schedule related to each department and centres and ask them to conduct the audit.		
(vii)	Give the list of records and documents to be kept ready in the department for the auditors.		
(viii)	Give sample questions to all concerned to be prepared for responding, if asked by the audit team.		
(ix)	Give the points in advance to be presented by the department in front of audit teams.		
(x)	Give the list of documents to be prepared by the departments during and after audit		
(xi)	Inform what type of information to be shared by the individuals during the academic audit.		

Sl. No.	*Statements*	*Rating*	*Comment, if any*
(xii)	Inform all individuals that which information adds marks to their quality and which does not.		
(xiii)	Prepare all Individual mentally and physically to accept the challenge of academic audit.		
(xiv)	Provide moral support to all concerned and assure not to worry, in case they found defaulter.		
(xv)	Any other.		
8.	**To implement academic audit system in the institution, the academic audit cell should be comprised of :**		
(i)	Representatives of trustees and management.		
(ii)	Selected academic committee members by management.		
(iii)	Representatives from other institutions.		
(iv)	Experts.		
(v)	Any other.		
9.	**The frequency of internal academic audit should be :**		
(i)	Monthly.		
(ii)	Quarterly.		
(iii)	Semester-wise.		
(iv)	Annually.		
(v)	Any other.		
10.	**The frequency of external academic audit should be :**		
(i)	Once in four years.		
(ii)	Once in three years.		
(iii)	Once in two years.		
(iv)	Once in a year.		
(v)	Semester-wise.		
(vi)	Any other.		

Sl. No.	*Statements*	*Rating*	*Comment, if any*
11.	**Academic audit system should be designed by :**		
(i)	A team comprising outside experts.		
(ii)	A team comprising of a few outside experts and internal trained members of the institution.		
(iii)	A team comprising trained institutional members only.		
(iv)	Any other.		
12.	**The frequency of refinement of academic audit system should be :**		
(i)	One year.		
(ii)	Two years.		
(iii)	Three years.		
(iv)	Four years.		
(v)	Any other.		
13.	**The academic audit should be conducted for inputs such as :**		
(i)	Ascertaining admission procedure of students.		
(ii)	Ascertaining entry behaviour of students.		
(iii)	Ascertaining quality of curriculum.		
(iv)	Ascertaining quality of recruitment process.		
(v)	Ascertaining quality of learning resources.		
(vi)	Ascertaining quality of training of faculty and staff members.		
(vii)	Ascertaining quality of classrooms facilities.		
(viii)	Ascertaining quality of resources in the laboratories.		
(ix)	Ascertaining quality of resources in the workshops.		
(x)	Ascertaining quality of resources in the library.		
(xi)	Ascertaining quality of training plan of faculty and staff members.		

Sl. No.	*Statements*	*Rating*	*Comment, if any*
(xii)	Ascertaining the procedures for purchase, use and discarding of printed modules and library books.		
(xiii)	Ascertaining the procedure for use and discarding of teacher's made modules, charts, handouts and reports.		
(xiv)	Ascertaining the procedure for purchase, use and discarding of non-pint (CD, cassettes, OHP slides, Power point) learning resources.		
(xv)	Ascertaining the procedure for career promotional policies for faculty members and staff.		
(xvi)	Any other.		
14.	**The academic audit should be conducted for processes such as :**		
(i)	Policies formulation.		
(ii)	Plans preparation.		
(iii)	Classroom teaching learning processes.		
(iv)	Laboratory teaching learning processes.		
(v)	Workshop and field experiences processes.		
(vi)	Curriculum implementation.		
(vii)	Instructional processes for achieving the course/subject objectives.		
(viii)	Lesson plan for all types of teaching learning methods such as lecture, demonstration, group discussions, panel discussions, focus group discussions, case method, seminar, conference, symposium, project, research, action learning, problem based learning, excursion visit, game, competition, role play, simulation, self learning, computer aided learning, e-learning, assignments, etc.		
(ix)	Laboratory experiment.		
(x)	Organizing industrial training and visits for faculty and student.		
(xi)	Real life project (major).		
(xii)	Assessment of learning.		

Sl. No.	Statements	Rating	Comment, if any
(xiii)	Learning resources development.		
(xiv)	Research work.		
(xv)	Co-curricular and extra curricular activities such as guidance, counselling, personality development, pursuing hobby etc.		
(xvi)	Performance appraisal of teachers and staff.		
(xvii)	Curriculum development, implementation and evaluation.		
(xviii)	Encouraging industries institutions interactions.		
(xix)	Making career avenues and campus interviews followed by placements for student.		
(xx)	Tracer study of the passouts.		
(xxi)	Physical stock verification of learning resources and equipment.		
(xxii)	Any other		
15.	**The academic audit should be conducted for outputs such as :**		
(i)	Certification.		
(ii)	Curriculum revision.		
(iii)	Training and development of faculty and staff members.		
(iv)	Learning resources revision and development.		
(v)	Any other.		
16.	**The duration of internal academic audit should be :**		
(i)	One day.		
(ii)	Two days.		
(iii)	Three days.		
(iv)	One week.		
(v)	Any other.		
17.	**The duration of external academic audit should be :**		

Sl. No.	*Statements*	*Rating*	*Comment, if any*
(i)	One day.		
(ii)	Two days.		
(iii)	Three days.		
(iv)	Any other.		
18.	**Prerequisite conditions for implementing academic audit in technical institutions are :**		
(i)	Zeal to give quality education to student.		
(ii)	Adequate faculty and staff members.		
(iii)	Competent faculty and staff members.		
(iv)	Commitment for quality of academic services.		
(v)	Autonomy to faculty and staff to experiment.		
(vi)	Competitive as well as conducive environment for enriched learning.		
(vii)	Commitment to acquire name, fame, image and excellence.		
(viii)	Self motivation and incentive scheme.		
(ix)	Any other.		
19.	**Internal academic audit should be conducted using ways and means of :**		
(i)	Interactions between faculty, staff, management, trustees and all stakeholders.		
(ii)	Meetings between faculty, staff, management, trustees and all stakeholders.		
(iii)	Workshop between faculty, staff, management, trustees and all stakeholders.		
(iv)	Any other.		
20.	**External academic audit should be conducted using ways and means of :**		
(i)	Interactions between faculty, staff, management, trustees and all stakeholders.		

Sl. No.	Statements	Rating	Comment, if any
(ii)	Meetings between faculty, staff, management, trustees and all stakeholders.		
(iii)	Workshop between faculty, staff, management, trustees and all stakeholders.		
(iv)	Any other.		
21.	**Results compiled after conducting academic audit should be informed to institutional members by way of :**		
(i)	Circulating academic audit report and recommendation.		
(ii)	Organizing series of meetings.		
(iii)	Sharing in workshops.		
(iv)	Any other.		
22.	**Faculty and staff members who do not strictly adhering to academic quality systems should be :**		
(i)	Offered positive and constructive feedback for making improvement in processes.		
(ii)	Counselled with mentioning benefits of quality systems and requesting to cooperate.		
(iii)	Provided more training to set target.		
(iv)	Given punishment with mentioning slackness.		
(v)	Given time to improve performance under guidance.		
(vi)	Given explanation and show cause notice.		
(vii)	Any other.		
23.	**Academic audit system designed by the institution should be :**		
(i)	Common for all the disciplines.		
(ii)	Different for different disciplines.		
(iii)	Common for common dimensions of audit and different for specific dimensions.		
(iv)	Any other.		

Sl. No.	*Statements*	*Rating*	*Comment, if any*
24.	**Results and recommendations of academic audit should be used for :**		
(i)	Rewarding high quality achievers.		
(ii)	Sharing success and failure for improvement.		
(iii)	Refinement of future academic audit system.		
(iv)	Setting the standards and benchmarks.		
(v)	Informing to all the stakeholders.		
(vi)	Publicizing and advertising the achievement of goals of the institution.		
(vii)	Distribution of incentives and bonus.		
(viii)	Any other		
25.	**Selection of internal auditors should be made using criteria such as :**		
(i)	Voluntary basis.		
(ii)	By the order of the director/principal.		
(iii)	Trained persons in academic audit.		
(iv)	Through qualifying test.		
(v)	Nominating individuals from management.		
(vi)	Any other		
26.	**Internal auditors should be given rewards for successfully organizing and conducting internal academic audit in the institution :**		
(i)	Cash prize.		
(ii)	Certificate.		
(iii)	Outside training opportunity.		
(iv)	More higher and challenging responsibilities in the institute looking to their interest.		
(v)	Role of their choice in the quality assurance.		
(vi)	Sponsorship for national and international programmes.		
(vii)	A grand title felicitation.		
(viii)	Any other		

Sl. No.	*Statements*	*Rating*	*Comment, if any*
27.	**The academic audit systems should be introduced in the institution by way of :**		
(i)	Organizing series of training programmes and workshops.		
(ii)	Circulars, orders and guideline documents designed by the experts.		
(iii)	Organizing grand ceremony		
(iv)	Newspaper publicity and press conferences		
(v)	Any other.		
28.	**What could be the potential problems in implementing academic audit in the institution :**		
(i)	Lack of commitment towards quality.		
(ii)	Fear among faculty and staff of being rejected if found unsuitable.		
(iii)	Less attention towards main work.		
(iv)	Fear from extra work related responsibility.		
(v)	Shortage of faculty and staff to conduct audit.		
(vi)	Faculty and staff members are not appropriately trained in providing quality education to the student.		
(vii)	Shortage of physical resources such as equipments in laboratory, machines, soft-wares, funds, useful learning resources and library books.		
(viii)	Lack of incentives and motivations to the faculty and staff members.		
(ix)	Any other.		
29.	**Academic audit should be based on :**		
(i)	Direct assessment of quality of academic processes		
(ii)	Evidences of adherences to quality processes.		
(iii)	Any other.		

Sl. No.	Statements	Rating	Comment, if any
30.	**Academic audit report should be :**		
(i)	Publicly announced.		
(ii)	Kept confidential and not for disclosures.		
(iii)	Disclosed to internal members and trustees.		
(iv)	Exhibited in the institution's exhibition.		
(v)	Made available to all the stakeholders.		
(vi)	Made available on institute's website.		
(vii)	Any other.		
31.	**Principles of academic audit should be :**		
(i)	Achieving quality goals as speculated in the earlier formulated vision, missions and strategic plan.		
(ii)	Universal responsibility of institutional members.		
(iii)	Commitment of management, faculty, staff and students to quality of education.		
(iv)	Use of scientific tools and techniques.		
(v)	Conducted with an objective of improvement in existing academic audit system and learning of students.		
(vi)	Integrated with implementation of processes.		
(vii)	Any other.		
32.	**Documents to be maintained for conducting academic audit :**		
(i)	Academic audit manual for conducting audit year-wise.		
(ii)	All plans of action.		
(iii)	All evidences of achieving quality at every stage in the system.		
(iv)	Computerization of records and evidences.		
(v)	Any other.		
33.	**What are the benefits of conducting formative and internal academic audit in the institution :**		
(i)	Immediate corrective actions possible.		

Sl. No.	Statements	Rating	Comment, if any
(ii)	Self-learning from review and constructive feedback.		
(iii)	Less chances to repeat the mistakes.		
(iv)	Sharing of experiences for educating others.		
(v)	Enrichment of quality culture.		
(vi)	Removal of confusion and conflicts.		
(vii)	Enchantment in accountability of faculty and staff members for quality.		
(viii)	Self-satisfying and rewarding.		
(ix)	Identification of training needs and organization of need based training programmes.		
(x)	Effective communication on quality issue.		
(xi)	Collective learning about quality.		
(xii)	Functional problems of the system are identified.		
(xiii)	Any other		
34.	**What are the benefits of conducting summative and external audit :**		
(i)	Identification of major strengths and weaknesses related to quality of learning at institution level.		
(ii)	Sharing of best practices followed by centre of excellence towards quality improvement.		
(iii)	Review and refinement of the academic audit system.		
(iv)	Institution-wise training and guidance.		
(v)	Base for taking major quality related policy decisions.		
(vi)	Any other.		
35.	**The auditors must possess competencies such as :**		
(i)	Design academic quality system.		
(ii)	Use scientific tools and techniques.		
(iii)	Commit to quality.		

Sl. No.	*Statements*	*Rating*	*Comment, if any*
(iv)	Prepare academic audit plan.		
(v)	Conduct academic audit as per plan.		
(vi)	Conduct discussions, interviews, workshop, etc.		
(vii)	Document audit information and results.		
(viii)	Draw conclusions.		
(ix)	Give appropriate reasons for each slackness.		
(x)	Prepare report for presentation.		
(xi)	Present report.		
(xii)	Provide constructive and positive feedback in a soft manner for improving quality of learning.		
(xiii)	Impart training in quality aspects.		
(xiv)	Any other.		
36.	**What could be the best mode of information gathering for knowing the progress made by conducting academic audit :**		
(i)	Organizing interviews in person.		
(ii)	Analysis of documents being maintained.		
(iii)	Focused group discussion on significant issues related to quality.		
(iv)	Organizing workshop.		
(v)	Organizing meetings.		
(vi)	Organizing paper presentation.		
(vii)	Noting the changes as observed by stakeholders.		
(viii)	Any other.		
37.	**Academic audit information can also be gathered from the sources such as :**		
(i)	Ongoing students.		
(ii)	Passouts students.		
(iii)	Employers of the passouts students.		
(iv)	Teachers.		

Sl. No.	*Statements*	*Rating*	*Comment, if any*
(v)	Stakeholders.		
(vi)	Director/principal.		
(vii)	Parents of ongoing and passout students.		
(viii)	Any other.		
38.	**What should be the terms of reference for external audit team for introducing academic audit system in the institution :**		
(i)	Participatively design academic audit system.		
(ii)	Prepare academic audit implementation manual.		
(iii)	Review academic processes in the light of best practices		
(iv)	Identify best practices.		
(v)	Identify quality gaps in academic processes.		
(vi)	Report the observations and offer constructive feedback for improvement.		
(vii)	Impart training to faculty and staff members.		
(viii)	Any other.		
39.	**What indicators of quality education be decided for judgements of a common men :**		
(i)	Demand for admission in the institution.		
(ii)	Name and fame of the institution.		
(iii)	Learned, high class, experienced faculty and staff members in the institution.		
(iv)	Better management control and discipline.		
(v)	All newer programmes in the town.		
(vi)	Good architecture of the building and learning environment.		
(vii)	Placement of students and their status.		
(viii)	Demand of the programme by students.		

Sl. No.	*Statements*	*Rating*	*Comment, if any*
(ix)	**High quality documentation.**		
(x)	**Quality assurance processes in place.**		
(xi)	**Scientific process of design of curriculum.**		
(xii)	**Frequency of revision of curriculum.**		
(xiii)	**Participation of industry, research institutions and professional bodies in curriculum development.**		
(xiv)	**Frequency of revision of instructional resources.**		
(xv)	**Development of new instructional resources.**		
(xvi)	**Variety in instructional resources.**		
(xvii)	**Design of lesson plans.**		
(xviii)	**Variety in use of instructional methods.**		
(xix)	**Demand driven programmes in collaboration with industry.**		
(xx)	**Systematic design and implementation of educational programme.**		
(xxi)	**Institutional members should be aware about academic processes.**		
(xxii)	**Any other.**		
40.	**Academic audit is different than NBA accreditation on parameters such as :**		
(i)	**It is conducted against the processes and parameters designed by the institution and not against the national standards.**		
(ii)	**It is a continuous process whereas the NBA accreditation is carried out once in five years or three years.**		
(iii)	**The NBA accreditation is carried out by an external team, whereas the academic audit is conducted by internal teams.**		
(iv)	**The institution has to spend some money on NBA accreditation but academic audit can be conducted without much expenditures.**		
(v)	**Academic audit is a process of empowerment of people for quality of learning whereas the NBA accreditation is a process of educating people for quality of learning.**		

Sl. No.	*Statements*	*Rating*	*Comment, if any*
(vi)	Academic audit is a quality assurance mechanism and quality graduates itself is a certificate whereas the NBA provides accreditation certificate which is a recognized document for maintaining minimum standards.		
(vii)	Any other.		
41.	**Academic audit is different than ISO on parameters such as :**		
(i)	Academic audit is conducted against the quality system designed to achieve the vision of the institution whereas the ISO guides to design the system.		
(ii)	Academic audit is conducted by internal and external members and same is the case with ISO.		
(iii)	ISO certificate is awarded by authorized agency whereas there is no need of any certificate in academic audit.		
(iv)	Both focuses on continuous improvement and enrichment in the instructional processes of learning.		
(v)	In both, the documentation and evidences are required to exhibit the performance.		
(vi)	Any other.		
42.	**Academic audit is different than performance appraisal on parameters such as :**		
(i)	Academic audit is related to performance of the processes against well-designed system whereas the performance appraisal is the assessment of the performance of individuals' and teams' against their respective plan.		
(ii)	The performance of the individuals and teams lead to quality of education in both cases.		
(iii)	The performance appraisal focuses on improving the performance of individuals and teams and harnessing their potential whereas the academic audit focuses on improving the quality of learning of students through improving the processes.		

Sl. No.	Statements	Rating	Comment, if any
(iv)	Performance appraisal could be a part of the academic audit.		
(v)	Any other.		

STRUCTURED QUESTIONS

The questions given below are related to the current status of academic audit in your institution and your role for assuring quality. Kindly, feel free to respond the questions. If necessary, use additional sheet for elaborating your responses.

1. Do you have formal academic audit system in your institution?
2. Have you received training on academic audit ? If yes, specify areas.
3. Are you interested in receiving training on academic audit ? If yes, specify areas.
4. How much time you can spare for academic audit training? Specify days, weeks etc.
5. Is academic audit a very new concept for you ?
6. Have you read literature on academic audit ? If yes, please give details
7. Have you visited any institution that has implemented academic audit ? If yes, name the institution and state significant observations made by you on quality assurance.
8. Would you like to initiate with your management to conduct an awareness level training programme on academic audit in your institution?
9. Will management of your institution implement the academic audit system in your institution ?
10. Will management of your institution provide resources to implement the academic audit system in your institution ?

Appendix-I

Formats

List of Formats for Academic Audit

Format	*Institutional level*
1.	Audit the recruitment process
2.	Audit the admission process of students
3.	Assess the entry behaviour of students
4.	Audit curriculum implementation plan
5.	Audit lesson plan
6.	Audit laboratory experiment plan
7.	Audit assessment scheme
8.	Audit lecture method
9.	Audit demonstration method
10.	Audit question answer (QA) method
11.	Audit group discussion
12.	Audit panel discussions
13.	Audit role play
14.	Audit simulation
15.	Audit game
16.	Audit in basket
17.	Audit students seminars
18.	Audit creativity sessions
19.	Audit assignments
20.	Audit quiz
21.	Audit action learning
22.	Audit practical
23.	Audit workshop practice
24.	Audit projects
25.	Audit exposure visit
26.	Audit reports
27.	Audit presentations
28.	Audit researches
29.	Audit continuing education programmes
30.	Audit training of faculty and staff

Format

Format 1: Audit—The Recruitment Process

Instructions for Auditors : Audit the recruitment process of faculty and staff members on criteria stated in the table given below. During the process of audit of recruitment process, if you come across deficiencies/gaps/weaknesses, note down the extent of gap in column 3 and description of the gap in column 4 of the Format given below. After examining the complete recruitment process against each criteria and noting down the deficiencies/gaps/weaknesses think about the strategies to bring improvements in the recruitment process on various criteria and note down the strategy in column 5. You can think about value additions with respect to the criteria under consideration even if you do not find any weakness and mention it in column 5. Please use following scale for indicating extent of deficiencies/gaps/weaknesses in column 3.

- 5 – indicates very high deficiency/gap/weakness,
- 4 – indicates high deficiency/gap/weakness,
- 3 – indicates medium deficiency/ gap/weakness,
- 2 – indicates low deficiency/gap/weakness,
- 1 – indicates very low deficiency/gap/weakness, and
- 0 – indicates no deficiency/gap/weakness.

Format 1.—Audit—The Recruitment Process

Sl. No.	*Criteria*	*Extent of deficiencies/ gaps/ weaknesses/ scope for improvement*	*Description of deficiencies/ gaps/ weaknesses/ scope for improvement*	*Strategies to bring improvement*
1	2	3	4	5
1.	Job/role description of the faculty and staff is prepared and updated considering the requirements of the institution			
2.	The requirement of faculty and staff is identified every year considering the business of the institution			
3.	The positions are advertised with job/role description at national level			

***Format 1* : Contd.**

Sl. No.	*Criteria*	*Extent of deficiencies/ gaps/ weaknesses/ scope for improvement*	*Description of deficiencies/ gaps/ weaknesses/ scope for improvement*	*Strategies to bring improvement*
4.	The applications are scrutinized according to needs of the institution and job/role needs			
5.	Competency of the candidate is tested for selection			
6.	The candidate is oriented about the institutional requirements and job/role			
7.	The candidate is tested on the job after orientation and feedback for improvement in performance is provided			
8.	The performance of the candidate is assessed for a year			
9.	Decision is taken for clearing the probation			
10.	Further training and development opportunities are created			

Format 2* : *Audit—The Admission Process of Students

Sl. No.	*Criteria*	*Extent of deficiencies/ gaps/ weaknesses/ scope for improvement*	*Description of deficiencies/ gaps/ weaknesses/ scope for improvement.*	*Strategies to bring improvement*
1	2	3	4	5
1.	Admission policy publicized in advance			
2.	Admission test aligned to programmes, valid and reliable is conducted			
3.	The test checking and assessment is fair			

(Contd.)

Format 2 : Contd.

Sl. No.	Criteria	Extent of deficiencies/ gaps/ weaknesses/ scope for improvement	Description of deficiencies/ gaps/ weaknesses/ scope for improvement	Strategies to bring improvement
1	2	3	4	5
4.	The result is declared as per admission policy			
5.	The students are admitted according to merit			

Format 3 : Audit—Entry Behaviour of Students

Sl. No.	Criteria	Extent of deficiencies/ gaps/ weaknesses/ scope for improvement	Description of deficiencies/ gaps/ weaknesses/ scope for improvement	Strategies to bring improvement
1	2	3	4	5
1.	Scientifically designed transparent process of assessing the entry behaviour of students for taking a programme/course			
2.	Objective criteria for assessing the entry behaviour of students for pursuing a particular programme/course			
3.	The students are encouraged to do strengths, weaknesses, opportunities and threat analysis			
4.	Students are guided to set the vision, ambitions, Aspirations according to their strengths and interest			
5.	Bridge courses are offered to fill up the gap to opt for a particular course			
6.	Opportunities to achieve the vision			
7.	Variety of methods are used to harness the full potential of students for learning and development			

(Contd.)

Format 3 : Contd.

Sl. No.	Criteria	Extent of deficiencies/ gaps/ weaknesses/ scope for improvement	Description of deficiencies/ gaps/ weaknesses/ scope for improvement	Strategies to bring improvement
1	2	3	4	5
8.	Students are grouped according to their preferences			
9.	Alternative course of actions are offered			
10.	Honest feedback is provided to students			

Format 4 : Audit—Curriculum Implementation Plan

Sl. No.	Criteria	Extent of deficiencies/ gaps/ weaknesses/ scope for improvement	Description of deficiencies/ gaps/ weaknesses/ scope for improvement	Strategies to bring improvement
1	2	3	4	5
1.	Training of teachers for implementing new/revised curriculum			
2.	The curriculum implementation plan is aligned to threshold competencies or job of the graduates in world of work			
3.	Lesson plan			
4.	Use of variety of instructional methods to create abundant learning opportunities for students			
5.	Use of variety of learning methods			
6.	Involvement of students in learning process			
7.	Clarity on teacher activities			
8.	Clarity on students activities			
9.	Planning of laboratory work			
10.	Planning of industrial training/projects			

Contd.

Format 4 : Contd.

Sl. No.	Criteria	Extent of deficiencies/ gaps/ weaknesses/ scope for improvement	Description of deficiencies/ gaps/ weaknesses/ scope for improvement	Strategies to bring improvement
1	2	3	4	5
11.	Provision for solving the students learning problems			
12	Method of record management			
13.	Time schedule			
14.	Assessment scheme			
15.	Method of providing feedback			

Format 5 : Audit—The Lesson Plan

Sl. No.	Criteria	Extent of deficiencies/ gaps/ weaknesses/ scope for improvement	Description of deficiencies/ gaps/ weaknesses/ scope for improvement	Strategies to bring improvement
1	2	3	4	5
1.	Instructional objectives			
2.	Linking with previous learning			
3.	Advance organiser			
4.	Development of lesson			
5.	Variety of instructional methods			
6.	Variety of learning resources			
7.	Questions to assess learning			
8.	Questions to stimulate thinking			
9.	Time schedule			
10.	Assignments			
11.	Assessment questions			

(*Contd.*)

Format 5 : *Contd.*

Sl. No.	Criteria	Extent of deficiencies/ gaps/ weaknesses/ scope for improvement	Description of deficiencies/ gaps/ weaknesses/ scope for improvement	Strategies to bring improvement
1	2	3	4	5
12.	Requirement of physical resources			
13.	Method of providing feedback			
14.	Flexibility in approach			
15.	Method of Summarization			
16.	Method of assessing learning			
17.	Advance information for next topic or learning event			

Format 6 : *Audit—The Laboratory Experiment Plan*

Sl. No.	Criteria	Extent of deficiencies/gaps/ weaknesses/ scope for improvement	Description of deficiencies/ gaps/ weaknesses/ scope for improvement	Strategies to bring improvement
1	2	3	4	5
1.	Instructional objectives			
2.	Linking with theory			
3.	Advance organizer			
4.	Type of experiments conventional, problem solving, project, research			
5.	Questions to assess learning			
6.	Time schedule			
7.	Assessment questions			
8.	Requirement of physical resources and their organisation			

(*Contd.*)

Format 6 : Contd.

Sl. No.	Criteria	Extent of deficiencies/gaps/ weaknesses/ scope for improvement	Description of deficiencies/ gaps/ weaknesses/ scope for improvement	Strategies to bring improvement
1	2	3	4	5
9.	Guidance and support to students			
10.	Diagnosing the learning problems			
11.	Assessment of learning and record keeping			
12.	Method of providing feedback			

Format 7: Audit—The Assessment Scheme

Sl. No.	Criteria	Extent of deficiencies/ gaps/ weaknesses/ scope for improvement	Description of deficiencies/ gaps/ weaknesses/ scope for improvement	Strategies to bring improvement
1	2	3	4	5
1.	Scientifically designed assessment scheme aligned to curricular objectives • Provision for formative and summative assessment • Provision for self, peer, teacher and expert assessment • Assessment integrated with learning process • Assessment assessing terminal competency			
2.	Written assessment scheme distributed			
3.	Objectivity in assessment			

(*Contd.*)

Format 7 : Contd.

Sl. No.	Criteria	Extent of deficiencies/ gaps/ weaknesses/ scope for improvement	Description of deficiencies/ gaps/ weaknesses/ scope for improvement	Strategies to bring improvement
1	2	3	4	5
4.	Transparency in assessment			
5.	Develops assessment skills in students			
6.	Scheduled			
7.	Timely declaration of results			
8.	Assessment guidelines mentioned			
9.	Assessment as a learning tool			
10.	Tools and techniques well designed			
11.	Emphasis on evidences			
12.	Provision for appeal			

Format 8 : Audit—Lecture Method

Sl. No.	Criteria	Extent of deficiencies/ gaps/ weaknesses/ scope for improvement	Description of deficiencies/ gaps/ weaknesses/ scope for improvement	Strategies to bring improvement
1	2	3	4	5
1.	Lesson plan			
2.	Link with previous learning			
3.	Advance organiser			
4.	Importance of learning relating to professional life and further learning			
5.	Quality of presentation—voice, clarity, link, richness in content body language, humour, movement, mannerism, time management, etc.			
6.	Use of media			

(*Contd.*)

Format 8 : Contd.

Sl. No.	Criteria	Extent of deficiencies/ gaps/ weaknesses/ scope for improvement	Description of deficiencies/ gaps/ weaknesses/ scope for improvement	Strategies to bring improvement
1	2	3	4	5
7.	Use of various instructional methods such as buzz group, question answer, classroom assignment, demonstration etc.			
8.	Use of principles of educational technology and educational psychology such as simple to complex, examples and non-examples, analogy, immediate feedback on learning progress etc.			
9.	Time provided for notes taking			
10.	Assessment of learning			
11.	Consolidation of learning			
12.	Questions			
13.	Information on next session			

Format 9 : Audit—Demonstration Method

Sl. No.	Criteria	Extent of deficiencies/ gaps/ weaknesses/ scope for improvement	Description of deficiencies/ gaps/ weaknesses/ scope for improvement	Strategies to bring improvement
1	2	3	4	5
A.	**Planning for demonstration**			
1.	Selection of method			
2.	Organisation of equipment			
3.	Size of the group and sitting arrangement			
4.	Appropriateness of place			
5.	Advance information to students on demonstration and learning from demonstration			

Format 9 : Contd.

Sl. No.	Criteria	Extent of deficiencies/ gaps/ weaknesses/ scope for improvement	Description of deficiencies/ gaps/ weaknesses/ scope for improvement	Strategies to bring improvement
1	2	3	4	5
B.	**Demonstration**			
6.	Distribution of learning resources			
7.	Overall information on demonstration			
8.	Sequence, connectivity and presentation relating it with theory and practice			
9.	Ensuring learning of students asking questions, inviting them to participate			
10.	Handling of equipment and implements			
11.	Creating opportunities for asking questions, sharing information, notes taking, curiosity etc.			
12.	Opportunity to students to repeat the steps			
13.	Time management			
14.	Precision in skills			
15.	Precision in attitudes			
16.	Command on subject and language			
C.	**Sum up**			
17.	Questions			
18.	Summarisation of learning			
19.	Establishing linkages with theory and practice			
20.	About next session			

Format 10 : Audit—Question Answer (QA) Method

Sl. No.	*Criteria*	*Extent of deficiencies/ gaps/ weaknesses/ scope for improvement*	*Description of deficiencies/ gaps/ weaknesses/ scope for improvement*	*Strategies to bring improvement*
1	2	3	4	5
A.	**Quality of Questions**			
1.	Aligned to learning objectives			
2.	Match with entry behaviour of students			
3.	Specific and clear			
4.	Stimulate learning and thinking			
5.	Diagnose learning problem			
6.	Increased order of difficulty			
7.	Challenging			
8.	Variety of questions			
9.	Conversational			
10.	Promote involvement of students			
11.	Shift responsibility of learning to students			
12.	Develop assessment skills in students			
13.	Sequence of questions			
14.	Ignite instinct to learn			
B.	**Organising question answer technique**			
15.	Well integrated with other methods of instruction			
16.	Quality of learning resources provided to students to learn			
17.	Effectiveness of exposure visit if it is based on the same			
18.	Support and guidance extended by teacher for finding the answer			

(*Contd.*)

Format 10 : Contd.

Sl. No.	*Criteria*	*Extent of deficiencies/ gaps/ weaknesses/ scope for improvement*	*Description of deficiencies/ gaps/ weaknesses/ scope for improvement*	*Strategies to bring improvement*
1	2	3	4	5
19.	**Conducive environment to ask or reply the question**			
20.	**Equal opportunity to students for participation**			
21.	**Level of reward, appreciation and recognition provided to students for correct answer**			
22.	**Level of encouragement to think on question**			
23.	**Level of diagnosing and filling the learning gaps**			
24.	**Level of handling the controversy, conflict and unnecessary discussion during the session**			
25.	**Level of curiosity, eagerness, anxiety and interest of students in QA sessions**			
26.	**Consolidation of learning by teacher**			
27.	**Appreciation of efforts of students**			
28.	**Fulfilment of learning objectives**			
29.	**Use of media and other learning resources**			

Format 11 : Audit—Group Discussion

Sl. No.	*Criteria*	*Extent of deficiencies/ gaps/ weaknesses/ scope for improvement*	*Description of deficiencies/ gaps/ weaknesses/ scope for improvement*	*Strategies to bring improvement*
1	2	3	4	5
A.	**Planning for group methods**			
1.	Appropriateness of method for achieving learning objectives			

Format 11 : Contd.

Sl. No.	*Criteria*	*Extent of deficiencies/ gaps/ weaknesses/ scope for improvement*	*Description of deficiencies/ gaps/ weaknesses/ scope for improvement*	*Strategies to bring improvement*
1	2	3	4	5
2.	Selection of problem, issue, theme, topic, decision requirement, strategy design etc.			
3.	Formation of group according to requirements of the skills, interest, level of competence, interest etc.			
4.	Size of the group			
5.	Criteria for assessment			
B.	**Introduce the situation to the group**			
6.	Written/video recorded description of the situation			
7.	Explaining/clarifying the situation			
8.	Expectation from the group members			
9.	Clarifying the criteria and method of assessment			
10.	Informing about the resources and time available			
C.	**Discussion on the situation**			
11.	Students discuss the situation and seek clarification if any and it is provided by the teacher			
12.	Control on discussion observing following points • Clarifying the situation • Selecting leader and reporter • Setting process of working • Focused discussion on situation			

Format 11 : Contd.

Sl. No.	Criteria	Extent of deficiencies/ gaps/ weaknesses/ scope for improvement	Description of deficiencies/ gaps/ weaknesses/ scope for improvement	Strategies to bring improvement
1	2	3	4	5
	• Participation of all the members			
	• Students applies previous learning in resolving situation			
	• Encouragement of divergent thinking			
	• Recording of discussion outcomes			
	• Drawing conclusions			
	• Opportunity for reflection on group process			
13.	Observing behaviour of individual members on well defined criteria mentioned in observation schedule			
14.	Draws sociogram			
15.	Guide for presentation			
D.	**Organising presentation session**			
16.	Invite groups for making presentation			
17.	Controls time of presentation			
18.	Summarizes learning points			
	• Connecting it with previous learning and theoretical learning			
	• Referring it to findings of different groups			
	• Recognition of good learning points			
	• Fill up gaps through additional inputs			
	• Connects it to further learning			
	• Responds to questions of students			

Format 11 : Contd.

Sl. No.	Criteria	Extent of deficiencies/ gaps/ weaknesses/ scope for improvement	Description of deficiencies/ gaps/ weaknesses/ scope for improvement	Strategies to bring improvement
1	2	3	4	5
	• Provide opportunity for reflection on learning • Provides constructive feedback on learning process			

Format 12 : Audit—Panel Discussion

Sl. No.	Criteria	Extent of deficiencies/ gaps/ weaknesses/ scope for improvement	Description of deficiencies/ gaps/ weaknesses/ scope for improvement	Strategies to bring improvement
1	2	3	4	5
1.	Selection of the topic aligned to instructional objectives			
2.	Comprehensiveness of instructions to students to prepare and participate in panel discussion			
3.	Level of preparation by students			
4.	Conduction of discussion			
5.	Participation of audience students in the forum discussion and question answer			
6.	Observation and assessment of learning of students participating in panel discussion by teacher, peer and students			
7.	Summarisation of learning by teacher			
8.	Positive and constructive feedback to panelist for improvement			
9.	Documentation of significant learning			

Format 13 : Audit—Role-Play

Sl. No.	*Criteria*	*Extent of deficiencies/ gaps/ weaknesses/ scope for improvement*	*Description of deficiencies/ gaps/ weaknesses/ scope for improvement*	*Strategies to bring improvement*
1	**2**	**3**	**4**	**5**
1.	Selection of role play aligned to instructional objectives			
2.	Plan to use role play			
3.	Instruction by teacher for role play			
	• Description of situation			
	• Allocation of role			
	• Setting for role play			
	• Expectations from role players			
	• Expectations from role observers (observation sheet)			
	• Time schedule			
	• Preparation time to role players			
4.	Enacting the role and observation by observers			
5.	Assessing the quality of activities on			
	• Skills demonstrated			
	• Mistake committed			
	• Skills not demonstrated			
6.	Experience sharing			
7.	Constructive and positive feedback for performing better role			
8.	Re-performance of the role			
9.	Consolidation of learning by teacher			
	• Linking learning with real life requirements			

(Contd.)

Format 13 : Contd.

Sl. No.	*Criteria*	*Extent of deficiencies/ gaps/ weaknesses/ scope for improvement*	*Description of deficiencies/ gaps/ weaknesses/ scope for improvement*	*Strategies to bring improvement*
1	2	3	4	5
	• Suggesting methods for refining the skills and attitudes			
	• Tips to all the students for observing the correct attitudes			
10.	Information on next role play			

Format 14 : Audit—Simulation

Sl. No.	*Criteria*	*Extent of deficiencies/ gaps/ weaknesses/ scope for improvement*	*Description of deficiencies/ gaps/ weaknesses/ scope for improvement*	*Strategies to bring improvement*
1	2	3	4	5
1.	Selection of simulation aligned to instructional objectives			
2.	Plan to use simulation			
3.	Instruction by teacher for simulation			
	• Description of simulation			
	• Precautions			
	• Risk involved			
	• Correct steps			
	• Check points			
4.	Performing in simulated conditions and observation by observers			
5.	Assessing the quality of performance on			

Format 14 : Contd.

Sl. No.	Criteria	Extent of deficiencies/ gaps/ weaknesses/ scope for improvement	Description of deficiencies/ gaps/ weaknesses/ scope for improvement	Strategies to bring improvement
1	2	3	4	5
	• Sequence and steps of performance			
	• Skills used			
	• Mistakes committed			
6.	Experience sharing			
7.	Constructive and positive feedback for better performance			

Format 15 : Audit—Game

Sl. No.	Criteria	Extent of deficiencies/ gaps/ weaknesses/ scope for improvement	Description of deficiencies/ gaps/ weaknesses/ scope for improvement	Strategies to bring improvement
1	2	3	4	5
1.	Selection of game aligned to instructional objectives			
2.	Plan to organise game			
3.	Brief instructions			
	• Participating teams			
	• Rules			
	• Conditions of performance			
	• Criteria for assessment			
	• Marks			
	• Time distribution			
4.	Organise game			
	• Resources			
	• Observers/judges			
5.	Assessing the learning on			
	• Skills demonstrated			

Format 15 : *Contd.*

Sl. No.	*Criteria*	*Extent of deficiencies/ gaps/ weaknesses/ scope for improvement*	*Description of deficiencies/ gaps/ weaknesses/ scope for improvement*	*Strategies to bring improvement*
1	2	3	4	5
	• Mistakes committed			
	• Skills not demonstrated			
6.	Experience sharing			
7.	Constructive and positive feedback for better learning			
8.	Consolidation of learning by teacher			
	• Linking learning with real life requirements			
	• Suggesting methods for refining the skills and attitudes			
	• Tips to all the students for designing strategies and observing the correct attitudes			
9.	Information about next game			

Format 16 : *Audit—In Basket*

Sl. No.	*Criteria*	*Extent of deficiencies/ gaps/ weaknesses/ scope for improvement*	*Description of deficiencies/ gaps/ weaknesses/ scope for improvement*	*Strategies to bring improvement*
1	2	3	4	5
1.	Design of in basket			
2.	Plan to organise in basket			
3.	Brief instructions			
	• Rules of in basket			
	• Learning from in basket			

(*Contd.*)

Format 16 : *Contd.*

Sl. No.	Criteria	Extent of deficiencies/ gaps/ weaknesses/ scope for improvement	Description of deficiencies/ gaps/ weaknesses/ scope for improvement	Strategies to bring improvement
1	2	3	4	5
	• Method of presentation • Conditions for performance • Criteria for assessment • Marks • Time distribution			
4.	Organise in basket • Preparation • Resources • Assessors			
5.	Assessing the learning on predefined criteria			
6.	Experience sharing			
7.	Constructive and positive feedback for better learning			
8.	Consolidation of learning by teacher • Linking learning with real life requirements • Suggesting methods for refining the skills and attitudes			
9.	Information about next in basket			

Format 17 : *Audit—Students' Seminar*

Sl. No.	Criteria	Extent of deficiencies/ gaps/ weaknesses/ scope for improvement	Description of deficiencies/ gaps/ weaknesses/ scope for improvement	Strategies to bring improvement
1	2	3	4	5
1.	Selection of issues/ problems/ themes for			

Format 17 : *Contd.*

Sl. No.	*Criteria*	*Extent of deficiencies/ gaps/ weaknesses/ scope for improvement*	*Description of deficiencies/ gaps/ weaknesses/ scope for improvement*	*Strategies to bring improvement*
1	2	3	4	5
	seminar aligned to instructional objectives			
2.	Brief instructions • Learning from seminar • Approach for completing the seminar • Reference and resource material • Behaviour to be demonstrated • Report preparation and presentation • Criteria for assessment • Marks • Time distribution			
3.	Plan to organise seminar			
4.	Guidance and support to students			
5.	Organise seminar • Preparation • Resources • Assessors • Question answer • Experience sharing			
6.	Constructive and positive feedback for better learning			
7.	Consolidation of learning by teacher • Linking learning with real life requirements • Suggesting methods for refining the skills and attitudes			
8.	Information about next seminar			

Format 18 : Audit—Creativity Sessions

Sl. No.	Criteria	Extent of deficiencies/ gaps/ weaknesses/ scope for improvement	Description of deficiencies/ gaps/ weaknesses/ scope for improvement	Strategies to bring improvement
1	2	3	4	5
1.	Selection of issues/ problems/ themes for creativity aligned to instructional objectives			
2.	Planning for creativity session • Welcome address • Sitting arrangement • Explanation of theme • Norms • Method of recording • Summarization • Time allocation			
3.	Organise creativity sessions			
4.	Organise creativity session • Welcome • Preparation of theme • Informing the norms • Organising resources • Creating conducive environment for creativity • Idea generation • Recording of ideas • Completing recording process • Combining & • classifying the ideas • Criteria for selecting ideas • Selecting ideas • Prioritizing ideas			

Format 18 : Contd.

Sl. No.	Criteria	Extent of deficiencies/ gaps/ weaknesses/ scope for improvement	Description of deficiencies/ gaps/ weaknesses/ scope for improvement	Strategies to bring improvement
1	2	3	4	5
	• Discussion of ideas for implementation			
	• Experience sharing on creativity			
5.	Constructive and positive feedback for better learning			
6.	Consolidation of learning by teacher			
	• Linking learning with real life requirements			
	• Suggesting methods for refining the skills and attitudes			
7.	Information about next creativity session			

Format 19 : *Audit—Assignments*

Sl. No.	Criteria	Extent of deficiencies/ gaps/ weaknesses/ scope for improvement	Description of deficiencies/ gaps/ weaknesses/ scope for improvement	Strategies to bring improvement
1	2	3	4	5
1.	Selection/design of assignment aligned to instructional objectives			
2.	Instructions to complete the assignments			
	• Explanation of assignment			
	• Method of completing and reporting			
	• Resource material			
	• Time allocation			

Format 19 : *Contd.*

Sl. No.	*Criteria*	*Extent of deficiencies/ gaps/ weaknesses/ scope for improvement*	*Description of deficiencies/ gaps/ weaknesses/ scope for improvement*	*Strategies to bring improvement*
1	2	3	4	5
	• Criteria for assessment			
3.	Provide guidance			
4.	Submission of assignment			
5.	Assessment of assignment and declaration of grades			
6.	Constructive and positive feedback for better learning			
7.	Collect sample assignments for record			

Format 20 : *Audit—Quiz*

Sl. No.	*Criteria*	*Extent of deficiencies/ gaps/ weaknesses/ scope for improvement*	*Description of deficiencies/ gaps/ weaknesses/ scope for improvement*	*Strategies to bring improvement*
1	2	3	4	5
1.	Matches with learning objectives			
2.	Stimulate spirit of competitiveness			
3.	Shift the responsibility of learning			
4.	Increases participation			
5.	Increases struggle			
6.	Develop healthy culture for learning			
7.	Produce by product learning			
8.	Briefing			
9.	Organized conduction			
10.	Debriefing			

Format 21 : Audit—Action Learning

Sl. No.	Criteria	Extent of deficiencies/ gaps/ weaknesses/ scope for improvement	Description of deficiencies/ gaps/ weaknesses/ scope for improvement	Strategies to bring improvement
1	2	3	4	5
1.	Design of action learning aligned to instructional objectives			
2.	Instructions to students to participate-Group, Resources, Time, Method and Norms			
3.	Organise • Clarify the topic • Inform interaction pattern • Provide opportunity for participation • Record ideas • Reflect on ideas • Generate solution or design innovations • Consolidate learning			
4.	Implement the solutions and reflect on implementation			
5.	Summarize and document the learning experiences			

Format 22 : Audit—Practical

Sl. No.	Criteria	Extent of deficiencies/ gaps/ weaknesses/ scope for improvement	Description of deficiencies/ gaps/ weaknesses/ scope for improvement	Strategies to bring improvement
1	2	3	4	5
1.	Planning of learning in Laboratory			

(Contd.)

Format 22 : Contd.

Sl. No.	Criteria	Extent of deficiencies/ gaps/ weaknesses/ scope for improvement	Description of deficiencies/ gaps/ weaknesses/ scope for improvement	Strategies to bring improvement
1	2	3	4	5
	• Guidelines and instructions to be followed			
	• Safety precautions			
	• Design of variety of experiments, assignments, demonstrations, manual			
	• Organisation of resources			
2.	Organise practical			
	• Information about learning events			
	• Group formation			
	• Performing practical by students			
	• Observation by teachers and instructors			
	• Guidance and support			
	• Feedback on performance			
	• Report writing			
	• Checking of report			
3.	Summarization of learning			
4.	Linking learning with theory and real life			
5.	Assessment of learning			
6.	Maintaining records			

Format 23 : *Audit—Workshop Practice*

Sl. No.	Criteria	Extent of deficiencies/ gaps/ weaknesses/ scope for improvement	Description of deficiencies/ gaps/ weaknesses/ scope for improvement	Strategies to bring improvement
1	2	3	4	5
1.	Planning of learning in workshop			
	• Guidelines and instructions to be followed			
	• Safety precautions			

Format 23 : Contd.

Sl. No.	Criteria	Extent of deficiencies/ gaps/ weaknesses/ scope for improvement	Description of deficiencies/ gaps/ weaknesses/ scope for improvement	Strategies to bring improvement
1	2	3	4	5
	• Design of variety of jobs • Organisation of resources			
2.	Performance • Group formation • Allocation of job • Job completion by students • Observation by teachers and instructors • Guidance and support • Feedback on performance • Report writing • Checking of report			
3.	Summarization of learning			
4.	Linking learning with theory and real life			
5.	Assessment of learning			
6.	Maintaining records			

Format 24 : *Audit—Projects*

Sl. No.	Criteria	Extent of deficiencies/ gaps/ weaknesses/ scope for improvement	Description of deficiencies/ gaps/ weaknesses/ scope for improvement	Strategies to bring improvement
1	2	3	4	5
1.	Decide the projects for students which are aligned to curriculum, selected from real life, challenging, integrate learning			

Format 24 : *Contd.*

Sl. No.	*Criteria*	*Extent of deficiencies/ gaps/ weaknesses/ scope for improvement*	*Description of deficiencies/ gaps/ weaknesses/ scope for improvement*	*Strategies to bring improvement*
1	2	3	4	5
2.	Assign the projects with clear instructions on; final outcome, format of project report, resources and time available for completing project, guidance and sup-port provided, assessment criteria and distribution of marks etc.			
3.	Submission of project plan by students and approval by teacher			
4.	Supervise the project • Discussions of students • Approach • Problem solving • Using resources • Participation • Performance • Learning • Preparation of project report • Submission of project report			
5.	Presentation on project			
6.	Assessment of learning			
7.	Consolidation of learning			
8.	Providing constructive feedback for further learning			

Format 25 : *Audit—Exposure Visit*

Sl. No.	*Criteria*	*Extent of deficiencies/ gaps/ weaknesses/ scope for improvement*	*Description of deficiencies/ gaps/ weaknesses/ scope for improvement*	*Strategies to bring improvement*
1	2	3	4	5
1.	Planning of exposure visit			

Format 25 : *Contd.*

Sl. No.	*Criteria*	*Extent of deficiencies/ gaps/ weaknesses/ scope for improvement*	*Description of deficiencies/ gaps/ weaknesses/ scope for improvement*	*Strategies to bring improvement*
1	2	3	4	5
	• Objectives • Industries • Duration • Permission			
2.	Instructions to students • For learning • For managing visit • Format of the report			
3.	Organise visit • Exposure • Notes taking • Recording the processes • Preparation of case studies, anecdotes, incidences • Interviewing			
4.	Preparation of report			
5.	Presentation of report and sharing experiences			
6.	Consolidation of learning			

Format 26 : *Audit—Reports*

Sl. No.	*Criteria*	*Extent of deficiencies/ gaps/ weaknesses/ scope for improvement*	*Description of deficiencies/ gaps/ weaknesses/ scope for improvement*	*Strategies to bring improvement*
1	2	3	4	5
1.	Format of report • Objectives • Rationale • Vision, mission, and goals			

Format 26 : Contd.

Sl. No.	*Criteria*	*Extent of deficiencies/ gaps/ weaknesses/ scope for improvement*	*Description of deficiencies/ gaps/ weaknesses/ scope for improvement*	*Strategies to bring improvement*
1	2	3	4	5
	• Organisational structure • Core business • Production and turnover • Quality of products and services • List of significant documents–manuals, charts, specification, processes performance appraisal • Significant learning in different sections—work, challenges, problems, wastage, specific things • Outcome of assignments • Case studies, incidences, anecdotes, and observations • Photographs • Conclusion • Appendix • Summary • Thanks			
2.	Report preparation • Logical • Simple • Attractive • Precise • Concise • Graphical • To the point			
3.	Oral presentation • Effective • Brief • To the point • Questions addressed			

Format 27 : Audit—Presentations

Sl. No.	*Criteria*	*Extent of deficiencies/ gaps/ weaknesses/ scope for improvement*	*Description of deficiencies/ gaps/ weaknesses/ scope for improvement*	*Strategies to bring improvement*
1	2	3	4	5
1.	Plan of presentation			
2.	Introduction of the assignment			
3.	Criteria for assessing presentation on main themes/ issues/ problem/ assignment			
	Content			
	(i) Depth and breadth of analysis			
	(ii) Examples and non examples			
	(iii) Innovativeness			
	(iv) Reference			
	(v) Logic			
	(vi) Clarity			
	(vii) Brevity			
	(viii) Questions handling of audience			
	Communication			
	• Voice			
	• Pitch			
	• Variation			
	• Body language			
	• Time management			
	• Diagrams, figures, charts etc.			
4.	Involvement of audience			
5.	Consolidation of learning by teacher			

Format 28 : Audit—Researches

Sl. No.	*Criteria*	*Extent of deficiencies/ gaps/ weaknesses/ scope for improvement*	*Description of deficiencies/ gaps/ weaknesses/ scope for improvement*	*Strategies to bring improvement*
1	2	3	4	5
1.	Guidelines for research study			
2.	Relevance of topics for research study			
3.	Clarity on research methodology			
4.	Guidance and support to students			
5.	Reference material			
6.	Procedure for assessing the thesis			
7.	Criteria for assessing the thesis			
8.	Constructive feedback for improvement			

Format 29 : Audit—Continuing Education Programmes

Sl. No.	*Criteria*	*Extent of deficiencies/ gaps/ weaknesses/ scope for improvement*	*Description of deficiencies/ gaps/ weaknesses/ scope for improvement*	*Strategies to bring improvement*
1	2	3	4	5
1.	Marketing of programmes and services			
2.	Training needs analysis • Role analysis • Problems • Future plans • Technological requirements • Performance level			

***Format 29 :** Contd.*

Sl. No.	*Criteria*	*Extent of deficiencies/ gaps/ weaknesses/ scope for improvement*	*Description of deficiencies/ gaps/ weaknesses/ scope for improvement*	*Strategies to bring improvement*
1	2	3	4	5
3.	Training programme design • Pre-test • Process sheet indicating contents, learning resources, learning method, assessment method, time, trainee activity etc. • Learning resources such as power point, transpare ncy, assignments, case study etc. • Post test			
4.	Variety of learning resources design			
5.	Programme conduction • Introduction and expectations of participants • Presentations • Assignments • Practice • Feedback • Assessment • Problem solving			
6.	Post test			
7.	Constructive feedback			
8.	Documentation of learning			

***Format 30 :** Audit—Training of Faculty and Staff*

Sl. No.	*Criteria*	*Extent of deficiencies/ gaps/ weaknesses/ scope for improvement*	*Description of deficiencies/ gaps/ weaknesses/ scope for improvement*	*Strategies to bring improvement*
1	2	3	4	5
1.	Training policy			

Format 30 : Contd.

Sl. No.	Criteria	Extent of deficiencies/ gaps/ weaknesses/ scope for improvement	Description of deficiencies/ gaps/ weaknesses/ scope for improvement	Strategies to bring improvement
1	2	3	4	5
2.	Training is linked with performance appraisal			
3.	Training needs of faculty and staff members are identified every year			
4.	In-house and outstation training plans are prepared			
5.	Training programmes are designed to satisfy the training needs			
6.	In-house training programmes are organized			
7.	Informal opportunities for training in the form of workshop, meetings, creativity sessions, seminars, panel discussions, experience sharing are frequently organised in planned manner			
8.	Institutional members are sponsored for outstation training programmes			
9.	Trained persons are provided opportunities to share the training experiences			
10.	Trained persons are provided opportunities to use skill developped through training			
11.	Impact of training is assessed on performance of the institution			

Summary

This book is a guide for development of academic audit system for higher and technical education institutions. This book contains 9 self-explanatory chapters with ample figures, models, guidelines, formats, instruments and activities. Glossary of terms is another speciality of this book.

Chapter 1 describes the concept, purposes, characteristics, and types of academic audit. It explains the difference between academic audit, accreditation, benchmarking and evaluation. It further details out assumptions for conducting academic audit, academic audit cycle, process of development of academic audit systems, process of conducting academic audit, code of conduct for auditees, tools and techniques for designing and conducting academic audit, frequency of academic audit, internal and external academic audit, auditors, documents maintained, formats, impact of academic audit on performance of the institution, recommendations based on academic audit, and guidelines to be followed by institution for effectively conducting academic audit.

Chapter 2 highlights the concept and power of vision, process of crafting vision and criteria for auditing the vision and process of vision.

Chapter 3 describes the concept, types and characteristics of organizational structure. It also explains the process of auditing the organizational structure.

Chapter 4 describes the hierarchy of plans, types of plans and process of auditing the plans and process of planning.

Chapter 5 explains the concept, characteristics, and purposes of curriculum. It describes the process of curriculum audit.

Chapter 6 explains the concept of case study and case method, and explains the process of case and case method audit.

Chapter 7 provides overview of industrial training, learning from industrial training, role of teachers and resource persons in organizing industrial training. It explains the process and criteria for auditing the industrial training.

Chapter 8 describes the concept, benefits, classification, and design of learning resources. It explains the concept of learning resources development, learning resources utilization and learning resources bank. The process and criteria for auditing the learning resources is explained.

Chapter 9 describes the emerging concepts, current status and trends of performance appraisal. The process and criteria for auditing the performance appraisal system are described in detail.

The instrument is given for assessing the awareness of faculty and staff members on academic audit. At the end of the book 30 formats are given to audit processes and outcomes.

Glossary

Accountability : The answerability of faculty and staff members to management of the institution for achieving the individual and institutional goals.

Accreditation : The quality of educational programmes of institutions is assessed and certified by statutory body using well-defined standards in the form of criteria and indicators using transparent process for stakeholders and general public. The process of accreditation is normally voluntary and it helps the institutions to enhance the quality of programmes to achieve the standards. It also entitles the institution for receiving government and non-government grants.

Appraisal : It is an interactive process of identifying the strengths and accordingly setting the goals and preparing the plans to use the strengths.

Assessment : It is a process of measuring the performance on well-defined criteria with reference to plan.

Autonomy : Students are provided freedom to learn and develop to their full potential creating opportunities for learning in the institution through curricular and co-curricular and extra-curricular activities. They are provided flexibility in choosing the competencies and courses of their choice, time, duration and method of learning. The students enjoy freedom, right and facilities of the institution for their own development. They get adequate opportunities in curriculum and course of study to choose a path of their interest and needs.

Benchmarking : It is a process of setting the qualitative and quantitative goals, processes and infrastructure for an institution with reference to best in that area. Generally, it is used for standards setting.

Best Practices : These are the methods, processes, models being implemented by the institutions for producing excellent result at a lower cost, time and efforts.

Brainstorming : It is a creativity technique used by resource persons to generate ideas on a particular aspect of quality or personality of a group of students or to solve a specific problem.

Competency Profile : It is a set of all types of competencies required to perform a particular role effectively and efficiently in present and near future which contributes significantly for achieving objectives related to core academic business of the institution.

Competency : The competency is a 'statement which describes the integrated demonstration of a cluster of related knowledge, skills, and attitudes that are observable and measurable, necessary to perform a role independently at a prescribed proficiency level.'

Continuous Improvement : It is the concept used in total quality management and other philosophy of management. It emphasizes that there should be improvement in the quality of graduates, products and services after completion of every cycle of performance. Considering the versatility of concept it is used for every management function like goal setting, process design, performance etc.

Core Competence : It is the capacity and capability of the organization to achieve the unique and different goals in competitive environment in successful manner at comparatively less cost, time, and efforts. It provides competitive leverage to the organization to deal with external environment.

Counselling : It is a psychological process to identify the behavioural problems of individuals and groups which are detrimental to academic business of the institution. The individuals are psychologically guided to remain abstain from such behaviour and perform according to set rules, norms and regulations.

Creativity Techniques : These are individual and group processes used by resource persons and teachers to generate new, different, unique and innovative ideas with reference to particular context. The creativity techniques are also used to develop thinking and creativity competencies/skills in students. There are numerous individual and group creativity techniques such as brain writing, cognitive mapping, idea writing, brain storming, nominal group techniques, delphi and the like that can be used by resource persons and teachers.

Creativity : It is a process of generating new, different and unique ideas for planning the career, problem solving and decision making, and strategy design. Creativity is considered as competency in engineering students and it is also used in proactive counselling.

Delight : This term is used to express the behaviour of the customers, beneficiaries and clients when they are served more than their genuine expectations.

Development : It is a process of identifying the needs, potential, ambitions and harnessing the same through education, training and practice for the satisfaction of the self and growth and development of the organization.

Effectiveness : It is related to setting right goals. In mathematical terms it is expressed as actual output divided by planned output.

Efficiency : It is an engineering concept. In mathematical terms it is expressed as output divided by input.

Enrichment : It is related to creating variety of opportunities for employees to use core competency in performing the role.

Evaluation : It is a systematic review of the impact of programme aims, competencies, learning processes, learning methods, supporting processes, learning resources, faculty and staff competency, supporting resources, etc. in order to take general and specific decisions to render it more purposeful, relevant, systematic, effective and efficient to satisfy and delight the stakeholders. It is a systematic process of collecting the data with a purpose to compare the current situation with expected or desired situation.

Feedback : The process of receiving information about the behaviour, progress on achievement of goals, quality of performance and method of performance. The information is received from various reliable sources and progress of the work.

Goals : These are the well defined quantitative and qualitative milestones for the organization, departments, teams and individuals for which they put their energy to reach the set destination.

HR Processes : All processes designed, implemented and evaluated to manage the employees of the institution. These processes are designed by HR managers and implemented by all managers.

Human Resources Development : It is a process of continuously improving the competence, capability and capacity of faculty and staff members of the organisation using proactive approaches of awareness, education, training and development endeavours.

Incentives : It is a kind of recognition provided to faculty and staff members for their performance up to the mark or more than that.

Innovation : It is a process of implementing creative ideas to achieve unique, different, novel and most desired objectives with minimum efforts, time and available resources.

Mission : The most desirous vision of the institution is achieved using mission statements in core areas of business derived from the vision of the institution. Mission statements express long-term milestones of development of the institution. These statements are useful in designing alternative strategies for development and influencing the stakeholders for extending guidance and support. The mission statements act as a source of encouragement for faculty and staff members.

Motivational Climate : The meaning of the motivational climate is related to inner urge to demonstrate the behaviour individually and collectively that is aligned to reaching the vision of the institution. Faculty and staff members are self-motivated to achieve day-to-day results keeping long-term objectives and goals in mind. Their energy is channelized and guided by the objectives they have in mind that are aligned to purposeful vision and mission of the institute. In many situations individuals and groups working in the institution become the source of motivation for each other. They spark the urge to do better for the institution.

Organizational Development : It is a process of diagnosing the current functioning of the institution in the light of expected performance and developing the human resources and other systems in order to achieve excellence.

Performance Appraisal : It is a system derived on the basis of strategic, perspective and tactical plan of the institution to develop the capacity and capability of teachers and staff members to implement the institutional plans to achieve the vision, missions, goals and objectives of the institution.

Personality : It refers to the organized, consistent, and general pattern of behaviour of a person which helps her/him to understand her/his behaviour as an individual.

Perspective Planning : It is a process of setting 3 to 5 years goals and designing strategies to achieve the same.

Policy : It is a broad statement that guides the decision making process or actions in the institution.

Potential : The personal capacity and capability of individuals and groups for achieving specific goals without much of efforts.

Proactive : It is a concept related to anticipating, visualizing, and predicting the future scenario based on limited information related to business to set the goals and design the strategies to achieve the same in planned manner.

Professional Approach : It is a process of proactively performing in the institution assuring quality of product and services without any waste of time efforts, money and energy and providing the instructional resources and academic services at right time in right quantity to students.

Professionals : These are the individuals and teams who perform in effective and efficient manner to achieve the institutional goals and objectives. Along with technical competencies they demonstrate professional competencies such as accepting the challenge, risk taking, working in a team, quick learning, problem solving, effective decision making, negotiating, collaborating, networking, working in uncertainty, predicting the future, visualizing the whole on the basis of available data, accepting accountability, managing change, coping with situation, influencing the customer, undertaking research and projects for quick response, adjusting in new environment and new culture, learning new and different competencies, forgetting fast, and so on. These competencies are different for different professions and different levels.

Proficiency : It is related to expected standard of performance and behaviour with reference to core academic business, quality of products and services, rules and regulations, working practices and processes of the institution.

Redeployment : The business of educational institutions is continuously changing in order to grab external opportunity for the growth and development of the institution and create new opportunities for the students. In changing environment the competencies and even manpower requirements at all levels may not match with the requirements of the core academic business. It is social responsibility of the institution to provide sustained employment to its faculty and staff members. In such situations the existing faculty and staff members are trained to develop new competencies which are needed to perform the changing academic business. These trained faculty and staff members are redeployed for new role.

Responsive : The institution identifies the changing needs of the students and stakeholders and accordingly offers the educational programme and services to always satisfy their needs. It also predicts the internal and external requirements related to curricular, co-curricular and extra-curricular and accordingly, reorganizes the processes.

Role Dimensions : These are the various aspects of role in which the position holders perform to satisfy the expectations of others and self. For example, a professor performs on various role dimensions such as teaching, learning resources development, research, consultancy, publication, curriculum design, assessment, administration, guidance and counselling and so on.

Role Enrichment : The role of the person is designed in such a way so that there is an opportunity for holding significant position, using variety of competency possessed, and freedom to plan the performance goals and implement strategies with a provision of internal as well as external feedback on the performance.

Role Significance : The important position assigned to a person in the institution is liked by that person and people get influenced by the performance of the person.

Role : The faculty and staff members fulfil the expectations of the internal and external members in the institution performing various tasks. The behaviour exhibited by the faculty and staff members during the performance is called role.

Satisfaction : This term is used to express the behaviour of the faculty and staff members when they get what they expect in terms of monetary, social and psychological rewards.

Self Actualization : It is the highest level of development of the individual.

Self Concept : It is the own assessment of individual about herself/ himself in a particular context.

Self Development : It is a systematic and conscious process identifying the needs, creating opportunities, and extending facilities to undergo various learning programmes for enhancing the ability, capability, competency, proficiency and commitment for excelling better for the benefit of the institution.

Stakeholders : The individuals and groups who influence the performance of employees in the institution or the employee can influence their performance.

Standards : The quantitative and qualitative values related to competencies and proficiency against which assessment and comparison is made.

Strategic Goals : The long term milestones the organization wants to achieve in order to achieve missions and vision of the institution.

Strategic Plan : It is written document prepared by every institution after going through rigorous planning exercises. It is prepared for 10 to 20 years. It is very broad in nature. It contains vision, missions, goals, and alternative strategies to accomplish vision of the institution. It provides base for preparing perspective and annual plans. It acts as a foundation for further planning process. The soundness of the strategic plan decides the future of the institution.

The Training Needs : These are defined in two contexts. First, it is defined in present context as the gaps in competency and proficiency level of the individual/team because of that they are not able to perform their role effectively and efficiently to meet performance standards although necessary resources required to perform the role are available in the organization. Second, it is defined in future context as the gaps perceived by the organization in the competency and proficiency level of the individual/team to perform potential roles in the organization. The standard competency profile is used for identifying the training needs.

Total Quality Management : It is a system developed in organization for sustaining, improving and expanding the scope of quality of educational programmes and services for satisfying and delighting the students and stakeholders.

Training : It is an opportunity created by the institution for its employees to develop themselves to self-actualization level in order to harness and use their full potential for the development of the institution and derive satisfaction out of it. It is imparted formally and informally to empower people to perform proficiently.

Value Addition : The systematic and scientific methods are used to enhance the quality of products and services of the institution. The value is added at input level, process level and output level to delight the students and make them cheerful. Various methods, media and information technology are used to add the value at each stage of functioning of the institution. Various methods such as suggestions, creativity, interview and common sense are used for adding value to learning process and services.

Values : Values serve as the foundation of relationship and the work for the institution. Values guide the work and relationship in the institution. These are expressed in terms of excellence, quality, concerns, customer satisfaction, community services, and commitment to contribute for new technology, self-development and so on.

Vision Reach Strategies : The institution, groups and individuals design a broad framework of efforts, resources and time to achieve the crafted vision.

Vision : It is the statement of future intents of institution that the institution wants to achieve in planned and professional manner. It is expressed in future expectations of the students, stakeholders and employees. It sets the aspirations and ambitions of the faculty and staff members. It provides the clear picture of the destination of the institution. It is always stated in positive and enduring terms. It bridges the gap between present and future. Many institutions are expressing it in quality and value loaded terms. The vision is never constrained by current limitations, capabilities, and capacities of the institution.

References

Earnest, Joshua (1997) – A Snap Study to Ascertain the Labour Market Orientation of the Competencies Required of Technicians. New Delhi: *The Indian Journal of Technical Education*; Vol. 20, No. 3.

Earnest, Joshua (2000) – Approaches to Competency-based Curriculum Development. New Delhi: *The Indian Journal of Technical Education*; Vol. 23, No. 4.

Earnest, Joshua (2005) – ABET Engineering Technology Criteria and Competency Based Engineering Education, *Proceedings of the 34th ASEE/IEEE Frontiers in Education Conference*; Indianapolis, USA; 19–22 October 2005

Finch, Curtis R. & Crunkilton, John R. (1993)–*Curriculum Development in Vocational and Technical Education – Planning, Content and Implementation*, Boston: Allyn and Bacon Inc.

Gupta, B. L. & Joshua Earnest (2008)–*Competency based Curriculum*, Mahamaya Publishing House, New Delhi.

Gupta, B. L. (2000)–Teams structure for polytechnics of 21st century, *The Indian Journal of Technical Education*, Volume 23, No. 2, April–June 2000, New Delhi.

Gupta, B. L. (2007)–*Governance and Management of Technical Institutions*, Concept Publishing Company, New Delhi.

Gupta, B. L. (2007)–*Management of Competency Based Learning*, Concept Publishing Company, New Delhi.

Gupta B. L. (2008)–*Management of Competency Based Training and Education*, Quality Publishing Company, Bhopal.

Gupta, B. L. (2009)–*Excellence Through Performance Appraisal*, Mahamaya Publishing House, New Delhi.

Ornstein, Allan C. & Hunkins, Francis P. (1988)–*Curriculum—Foundations, Principles and Issues*. Boston: Allyn and Bacon.

Wiles, Jon & Bondi, Joseph (1989)–*Curriculum Development—A Guide to Practice*. New York: Merrill Publishing Co.

Index